Writing
the Australian
Crawl

DATE DUE

2014	
JAN 16 2017	
2/6/18	F/uh
	PRINTED IN U.S.A.

POETS ON POETRY

David Lehman, General Editor
Donald Hall, Founding Editor

New titles

John Ashbery, *Selected Prose*
Annie Finch, *The Body of Poetry*
Alice Notley, *Coming After*
Charles Simic, *Memory Piano*

Recently published

Dana Gioia, *Barrier of a Common Language*
Paul Hoover, *Fables of Representation*
Philip Larkin, *Further Requirements*
William Stafford, *The Answers Are Inside the Mountains*
Richard Tillinghast, *Poetry and What Is Real*

Also available are collections by

A. R. Ammons, Robert Bly, Philip Booth, Marianne Boruch,
Hayden Carruth, Amy Clampitt, Douglas Crase, Robert Creeley,
Donald Davie, Thomas M. Disch, Tess Gallagher, Linda Gregerson,
Allen Grossman, Thom Gunn, Rachel Hadas, John Haines,
Donald Hall, Joy Harjo, Robert Hayden, Edward Hirsch,
Daniel Hoffman, Jonathan Holden, John Hollander, Andrew Hudgins,
Josephine Jacobsen, Mark Jarman, Galway Kinnell, Kenneth Koch,
John Koethe, Yusef Komunyakaa, Maxine Kumin,
Martin Lammon (editor), Philip Larkin, David Lehman, Philip Levine,
Larry Levis, John Logan, William Logan, William Matthews,
William Meredith, Jane Miller, David Mura, Carol Muske,
Geoffrey O'Brien, Gregory Orr, Alicia Suskin Ostriker, Ron Padgett,
Marge Piercy, Anne Sexton, Karl Shapiro, Charles Simic,
William Stafford, Anne Stevenson, May Swenson, James Tate,
Richard Tillinghast, C. K. Williams, Alan Williamson, Charles Wright,
James Wright, and Stephen Yenser

Writing the Australian Crawl

Views on the Writer's Vocation

WILLIAM STAFFORD

Ann Arbor   The University of Michigan Press

Copyright © by the University of Michigan 1978
All rights reserved
Published in the United States of America by
The University of Michigan Press
Manufactured in the United States of America
⊖ Printed on acid-free paper

2009   2008   2007   2006   23   22   21   20

Library of Congress Cataloging-in-Publication Data

Stafford, William Edgar, 1914–
      Writing the Australian crawl.

      (Poets on poetry)
      1. Poetry—Addresses, essays, lectures.
I. Title.   II. Series.
PN 1064.S77   1997   808.1   77-5711
ISBN 0-472-87300-8
ISBN 978-0-472-87300-5

Acknowledgments

Grateful acknowledgment is made to the following publishers, journals, and associations for permission to reprint adaptations, excerpts, and selections from copyrighted material:

Agenda for "The Practice of Composing in Language," *Agenda* 2, nos. 2-3 (Spring-Summer 1973).

American Poetry Review for "Finding What the World is Trying to Be," *American Poetry Review* 4, no. 4.

Bobbs-Merrill Company for "Making a Poem / Starting a Car on Ice." Reprinted from *American Poetry 1976*, edited by William Heyen. Bobbs-Merrill Company, 1976.

Brockport Writers Forum for "I Would Also Like to Mention Aluminum," edited from a video-tape interview with William Stafford in April 1974, sponsored by the Brockport Writers Forum, Department of English, State University College, Brockport, New York 14420 © State University of New York.

Conference of College Teachers of English of Texas for "The End of the Golden String," *Proceedings, CCTE* 38 (September 1973).

Field for "A Way of Writing," *Field*, no. 2 (Spring 1970).

Iowa Review for "Dreams to Have: An Interview with Cynthia Lofsness," *Iowa Review* 3 (Summer 1972).

Preface

The parts included here grew diversely. Some were written to order for publication—"A Way of Writing," written for *Field*, is an example. Some were remarks put together for conferences and then published in such places as *The Journal of the Conference on College Composition and Communication*. An example here is "Writing the Australian Crawl." One piece came from dreaming about having to speak, unprepared, before a critical audience: "What It Is Like."

It seems all right to me if the pieces eddy around recurrent topics and bring up issues roughed around in other pieces. I have smoothed the texts only where past circumstances had dictated wording that would be distracting or misleading in the present context.

Besides the guidance we all interchange as students, friends, and teachers, there is another kind of aid I want to acknowledge here: the interviews included have woven into them the presence and sustaining company of several who created the product and enlivened the doing. I'm thinking of how steady and intense and intelligent was the guidance when Sanford Pinsker and I harangued a tape recorder at Franklin and Marshall College one evening. And there were the deft moves at Brockport when William Heyen and Al Poulin swooped and gathered in many a topic, even including aluminum.

Contents

I. Background, *Sententia*

    What It Is Like   3

       Introduction to *Since Feeling Is First*   *4*

    A Statement on Life and Writings   9

    Writing and Literature: Some Opinions   12

II. Let Me Explain: Articles

    A Way of Writing   17

    Writing the Australian Crawl   21

    Capturing "People of the South Wind"   29

    The End of a Golden String   35

    Writing: The Discovery of Daily Experience   46

    The Practice of Composing in Language   52

    Some Arguments Against Good Diction   56

    Making a Poem / Starting a Car on Ice   61

    Whose Tradition?   76

III. Indirections: Interviews, Conversations

Dreams To Have: An Interview
with Cynthia Lofsness   85

Finding What the World Is Trying To Be:
An Interview with Sanford Pinsker   114

I Would Also Like To Mention Aluminum:
An Interview with William Heyen
and Al Poulin   127

IV. Toward This Book

Into the Cold World: Leaving the Workshop   157

I
Background, *Sententia*

What It Is Like

Poetry is the kind of thing you have to see from the corner of your eye. You can be too well prepared for poetry. A conscientious interest in it is worse than no interest at all, as I believe Frost used to say. It's like a very faint star. If you look straight at it you can't see it, but if you look a little to one side it is there.

If people around you are in favor, that helps poetry to *be*, to exist. It disappears under disfavor. There are things, you know, human things, that depend on commitment; poetry is one of those things. If you analyze it away, it's gone. It would be like boiling a watch to find out what makes it tick.

If you let your thought play, turn things this way and that, be ready for liveliness, alternatives, new views, the possibility of another world—you are in the area of poetry. A poem is a serious joke, a truth that has learned *jujitsu*. Anyone who breathes is in the rhythm business; anyone who is alive is caught up in the imminences, the doubts mixed with the triumphant certainty, of poetry.

INTRODUCTION TO
Since Feeling Is First

When language breaks loose like this—

> Now that the moon is out of a job, it has an easy climb,
> autumn nights, over empty farms where a family could live,
> or down city streets, or wide over the forest—all the still
> violins before they are carved—, on those paths only air ever
> uses. . . .

—when it rambles along with words and pictures homogenized in the mind's blender, strange things happen. Lines on the page may blunder into each other's sound, and even modern readers may follow their breath into paths our parents followed before we were born.

It is as if the ordinary language we use every day has in it a hidden set of signals, a kind of secret code. That code can touch into life a pattern in our feelings, a pattern not ordinarily roused by events that just *happen*, because what just happens is too random to bring about sustained feelings. But some language may start experiences that resonate with the self, with the being we have become amidst our apparently random encounters with this alien world.

Poems don't just happen. They are luckily or stealthily related to a readiness within ourselves. When we read or hear them, we react. We aren't just supposed to react—any poem that asks for a dutiful response is masquerading as a poem, not being one. A good rule is—don't respond unless you have to. But when you find you do have a response—trust it. It has a meaning.

Introduction to James Mecklenberger and Gary Simmons, *Since Feeling Is First* (New York: Scott Foresman, 1971).

About that lucky or stealthy quality in poems, it is easier to assert that there must be some profound relation between the reader and the poem than it is to prove what that relation is; for human responses may be teased forth so originally, so variously, that we do not need to know at first—nor do we actually have to be sure, ever—what the connections "really" are. The important thing is the feeling, not the points that we can list to account for how we feel.

For a poem is not the end, but the beginning, of an excursion. Back and forth we go—scenes, impressions, ideas. All sorts of quick glimpses occur to a hearer or reader. Some of those glimpses are quickly dismissed as random or uninteresting, but some lead richly onward. And the initial attitude toward those reading-glimpses is an attitude of welcoming: there must be some reason for whatever occurs to you. So, if you behave alertly and readily, as did the writer, you will not dismiss your own ideas, your own pictures, your own puzzlement; you will engage willingly with the events that occupy your mind, even the events that at first appear to be trivial or odd. Those mental events are primary, and all explanations must accommodate to them, not the other way round.

You could look at reading a poem this way: if you are thinking and there is a window nearby, you may look out—far. Your thinking will connect now and then to the scene, whenever something out there strikes your attention. Or, even more aptly, you might have a friend with you, and you would interchange, offer beginnings, slanted ideas, linked progressions. There would be a series of mental incidents, not predictable, never to be fully anticipated without the experience that comes about through following the sequence onward, point by point. Your experience would be richer—more would happen—than if you had been alone.

Reading is like that. It is not all your own ideas, and not all the other person's ideas. You toss back and forth against a live backboard. And, particularly if it is a congenial poem—or friend—you are reading or hearing, you furnish a good half of the life. The travel circuit of an idea or impression is a sequence of reboundings between you and the companion, between you and the page.

In these pages that follow, the poems do some rebounding among themselves; often one leads to another, and ricochets onward. And the pictures relate, sometimes oddly or in a reverse way, with the poems and with each other.

When you glance through these poems and pictures, you see many things that are not *good*; there are pains and oddities and startling images. Poems are not just about what is good; they can confront anything—anything. The variousness of the whole world springs out of a collection of poems—city, barred windows, Indians in the West, fields, forest, mountains, a man on a hammock at a farm in Minnesota. And through the ripple of attention and the shifting of memory and foresight, all will blend and reflect and enrich.

Take the man on the hammock at the farm in Minnesota: he hears and sees and feels a set of particular things; the whole experience is in a certain place, at a certain time, with a variety of local elements, some of them a kind usually neglected or accounted trivial. They are all brought clear and immediate. Then, abruptly, the poet turns to a summary conclusion that appears to leap uncalled for from the scene. But the conclusion is as much a real part of the scene as anything else mentioned. It is part of what happens.

And even more unfolds from the poem. The last line echoes another poet in another land, straying across this same mental terrain, through different circumstances. Linked with the poem in this book, the "wasted life" theme is reinforced by a picture of a wasted life—lethally wasted, an animal hanging from a barbed-wire fence on a farm. Then in the same direction, with further effect, another poem, "The Gallows," clenches on the theme—

> And many other beasts,
> And birds, skin, bone, and feather,
> . . .
> To swing and have endless leisure
> In the sun and in the snow,
> Without pain, without pleasure,
> On the dead oak tree bough.

No other picture-poem set in the book has that same kind of relation; other sets move on their own ways. They will not stay still for standard analysis. And this variety of effect implies something else: no text will say exactly what you want, or what anyone wants. No poem can be tame, *be good*. It acts up. Reverses occur—the pictures and the poems won't allow a reader to accept or reject passively. Participation is necessary.

In a sense, poems are not even fair. For instance, they do not always assert what they mean. And the same for pictures. A reader must get meaning through an action, through an act of response. And there are endless combinations of irony possible, and reversals, and second thoughts, and adjustments. Images and words put near each other begin to interact. What a poem says, it keeps on saying, with variations, to any being who keeps on saying and judging too, in his own way.

And a whole book in a larger pattern bears its echoes back and forth. One part may begin to resound from a remote place, across many pages, to an awakened recollection. The first picture in this book provides an example: a girl screams out through the bars; and then far along among the poems someone says, "I sit and look out. . . ." From that long reach between picture and text, from the turn of attention forced on a reader who follows and judges for himself, there come both torque and balance. The girl screams; the person who sits and looks out says, "I . . . see, hear, and am silent." But he *says* it, and in the saying, he has not wasted his life. He has made a move.

Now it is your move.

A Statement on Life and Writings

Our family is from Kansas, the middle of it, where I was born. We moved from one little town to another during my school years, following my father's jobs, which varied, but always provided income for our needs and books. We liked the towns and countryside, where we fished, hunted, and camped along the mild, wandering streams. Our lives were quiet and the land was very steady. Our teachers were good. Not till I finished my BA degree at the University of Kansas and went on to graduate school in another state did I ever see an adult drunk or enraged or seriously menacing. Higher education and the coming of World War II supplied a new aspect of experience.

As a pacifist I was in camps for conscientious objectors from 1940 till 1944. We fought forest fires, built trails and roads, terraced eroding land, etc. My brother was in the Air Force, and my sister married a Navy man. My service took me to Arkansas, then to California, then Illinois, where I worked finally in the headquarters of the Church of the Brethren. After the war I worked for Church World Service (a relief organization), and then by means of part-time college training got into college teaching. By 1948 I had a job teaching English at Lewis and Clark College in Portland, Oregon, where I still work. On occasion I have taught short intervals elsewhere and have even ventured on brief lecture and reading tours.

Earlier, encouraged by teachers in high school and college, I had attempted to write pleasing things; and while in camp during the war I found myself drawn to write meandering sequences of thoughts, or spun-out patterns of words, before the stove late, or in the early morning before work and before anyone else was stirring. This daily practice I have kept up ever since, and the pattern established then prevails as my way to write—during a quiet interval, without felt obligation to do other than find my way from impulse to impulse. I feel ready to follow even the most trivial hunch, and my notes to myself are full of beginnings, wavery hints, all kinds of inconclusive sequences sustained by nothing more than my indulgent realization that if it occurred to me it might somehow be justified. Now and then a sequence appeals to me for long enough to be teased into something like a poem, and when I feel sufficient conviction, I detach it from the accumulated leaves— my compost heap—and halfheartedly send it around to editors. I never feel sure that I have anything worthy, though I often feel affection for these products; and of all my writing only a very small portion goes forth into the world, and of that portion a large part never receives an editor's approval. I suppose at least nine out of ten pieces which I surmise to be poems find themselves coming home permanently to roost.

The pieces that have met approval appear in a wide variety of periodicals in the United States and in a few publications in England; and four main collections have appeared: *Traveling Through the Dark, The Rescued Year, Allegiances,* and *Someday, Maybe.*

It pleases me that my wife and four children hardly

know when these poems spring into being in our house, early and late. The family now and then will see a new book and thus be reminded that these writings are always waiting, and that I am receiving them and placing them with care all around us.

Writing and Literature

Some Opinions

A writer is a person who enters into sustained relations with the language for experiment and experience not available in any other way.

An editor is a friend who helps keep a writer from publishing what should not be published.

A reader is a person who picks up signals and enters a world in language under the guidance of an earlier entry made by a writer.

Literature is not a picture of life, but is a separate experience with its own kind of flow and enhancement.

Anyone enters that world of writing or literature by writing or reading, venturing forward part by part, unpredictable part by unpredictable part.

So flowing and ongoing is this way of entry that one could become a writer merely by little additions to ordinary language—adding a paragraph to each letter you normally write could lead you by little steps into increments of correspondence and induct you into a writing career.

The literary world is a community in that one interchanges with others naturally and becomes an insider, not by deals and stealth, but by a natural engagement with the ongoing work of other writers, editors, and publishers.

What one has written is not to be defended or valued, but abandoned: others must decide significance and value.

II
Let Me Explain
Articles

A Way of Writing

A writer is not so much someone who has something to say as he is someone who has found a process that will bring about new things he would not have thought of if he had not started to say them. That is, he does not draw on a reservoir; instead, he engages in an activity that brings to him a whole succession of unforeseen stories, poems, essays, plays, laws, philosophies, religions, or—but wait!

Back in school, from the first when I began to try to write things, I felt this richness. One thing would lead to another; the world would give and give. Now, after twenty years or so of trying, I live by that certain richness, an idea hard to pin, difficuit to say, and perhaps offensive to some. For there are strange implications in it.

One implication is the importance of just plain receptivity. When I write, I like to have an interval before me when I am not likely to be interrupted. For me, this means usually the early morning, before others are awake. I get pen and paper, take a glance out of the window (often it is dark out there), and wait. It is like fishing. But I do not wait very long, for there is always a nibble—and this is where receptivity comes in. To get started I will accept anything that occurs to me.

Something always occurs, of course, to any of us. We can't keep from thinking. Maybe I have to settle for an immediate impression: it's cold, or hot, or dark, or bright, or in between! Or—well, the possiblities are endless. If I put down something, that thing will help the next thing come, and I'm off. If I let the process go on, things will occur to me that were not at all in my mind when I started. These things, odd or trivial as they may be, are somehow connected. And if I let them string out, surprising things will happen.

If I let them string out. . . . Along with initial receptivity, then, there is another readiness: I must be willing to fail. If I am to keep on writing, I cannot bother to insist on high standards. I must get into action and not let anything stop me, or even slow me much. By "standards" I do not mean "correctness"—spelling, punctuation, and so on. These details become mechanical for anyone who writes for a while. I am thinking about such matters as social significance, positive values, consistency, etc. I resolutely disregard these. Something better, greater, is happening! I am following a process that leads so wildly and originally into new territory that no judgment can at the moment be made about values, significance, and so on. I am making something new, something that has not been judged before. Later others—and maybe I myself—will make judgments. Now, I am headlong to discover. Any distraction may harm the creating.

So, receptive, careless of failure, I spin out things on the page. And a wonderful freedom comes. If something occurs to me, it is all right to accept it. It has one justification: it occurs to me. No one else can guide me. I must follow my own weak, wandering, diffident impulses.

A strange bonus happens. At times, without my

insisting on it, my writings become coherent; the successive elements that occur to me are clearly related. They lead by themselves to new connections. Sometimes the language, even the syllables that happen along, may start a trend. Sometimes the materials alert me to something waiting in my mind, ready for sustained attention. At such times, I allow myself to be eloquent, or intentional, or for great swoops (Treacherous! Not to be trusted!) reasonable. But I do not insist on any of that; for I know that back of my activity there will be the coherence of my self, and that indulgence of my impulses will bring recurrent patterns and meanings again.

This attitude toward the process of writing creatively suggests a problem for me, in terms of what others say. They talk about "skills" in writing. Without denying that I do have experience, wide reading, automatic orthodoxies and maneuvers of various kinds, I still must insist that I am often baffled about what "skill" has to do with the precious little area of confusion when I do not know what I am going to say and then I find out what I am going to say. That precious interval I am unable to bridge by skill. What can I witness about it? It remains mysterious, just as all of us must feel puzzled about how we are so inventive as to be able to talk along through complexities with our friends, not needing to plan what we are going to say, but never stalled for long in our confident forward progress. Skill? If so, it is the skill we all have, something we must have learned before the age of three or four.

A writer is one who has become accustomed to trusting that grace, or luck, or—skill.

Yet another attitude I find necessary: most of what I write, like most of what I say in casual conversation, will not amount to much. Even I will realize, and even at the time, that it is not negotiable. It will be like practice. In conversation I allow myself random remarks —in fact, as I recall, that is the way I learned to talk— so in writing I launch many expendable efforts. A result of this free way of writing is that I am not writing for others, mostly; they will not see the product at all unless the activity eventuates in something that later appears to be worthy. My guide is the self, and its adventuring in the language brings about communication.

This process-rather-than-substance view of writing invites a final, dual reflection:

1. Writers may not be special—sensitive or talented in any usual sense. They are simply engaged in sustained use of a language skill we all have. Their "creations" come about through confident reliance on stray impulses that will, with trust, find occasional patterns that are satisfying.

2. But writing itself is one of the great, free human activities. There is scope for individuality, and elation, and discovery, in writing. For the person who follows with trust and forgiveness what occurs to him, the world remains always ready and deep, an inexhaustible environment, with the combined vividness of an actuality and flexibility of a dream. Working back and forth between experience and thought, writers have more than space and time can offer. They have the whole unexplored realm of human vision.

Writing the Australian Crawl

Our daughter Kit, six years old, stands by the lighted dashboard talking to Daddy as he drives home from a family trip to the beach. The others have gone to sleep, and Kit is helping—she talks to keep me awake. The road winds ahead, and she bubbles along, composing with easy strokes, imagining a way of life for the two of us.

> We'd have a old car, the kind that gets
> flat tires, but inside would be wolfskin
> on the seats and warm fur on the steering
> wheel, and wolf fur on all the buttons. And
> we'd live in a ranch house made out of
> logs with a loft where you sleep, and you'd
> walk a little ways and there'd be the farm
> with the horses. We'd drive to town, and
> we'd have flat tires, and be sort of old.

This artless bit of talk is a cue for my contention that the writer, like the talker who finds his best subject and responds eagerly with his whole self, can easily pour out a harmonious passage; writing, like talk, can be easy, fast, and direct; it can come about through the impulsive following of interest, and its form and proportion can grow from itself in a way that appears easy and natural.

To some, this contention of mine is weak; but as a teacher and writer I want to mark as clearly as possible a difference with many of my colleagues. Often when my friends pronounce responsibly about the values of creative work I experience a loss of contact. I want at such times to voice what may appear to be an antagonism, maybe even a willful stupidity, about "culture." To "learn the tools of writing," to "understand the essentials of the craft," to "base my practice on models that have proved to be fundamentally sound"—these apparently winsome and admirable phrases put me in a bleak mood. When I write, grammar is my enemy; the materials of my craft come at me in a succession of emergencies in which my feelings are ambivalent; I do not have any commitments, just opportunities. Not the learning of methods, not the broadening of culture, not even the preserving of civilization (there may be greater things than civilizations), but a kind of dizzying struggle with the Now-ness of experience, that is my involvement in writing. And I believe it is this interaction between imagination and its embodiment as it develops which sustains the speaker and the writer—and sustains the artist in other materials.

It is strange to me that we can come to accept the idea that language is primarily learned as speech, is soaked up by osmosis from society by children—but that we then assume the writing down of this flexible language requires a study of linguistics, a systematic checking with lists of standard practices, and so on. Now I realize that we possess many canned arguments about prescription *versus* description, and we share many nuances on this subject, from having written and talked about this topic; but I want to take a definite position, and my main plea is for the value of an unafraid, face-down, flailing, and speedy process in using the language.

Just as any reasonable person who looks at water, and passes a hand through it, can see that it would not hold a person up; so it is the judgment of commonsense people that reliance on the weak material of students' experiences cannot possibly sustain a work of literature. But swimmers know that if they relax on the water it will prove to be miraculously buoyant; and writers know that a succession of little strokes on the material nearest them—without any prejudgments about the specific gravity of the topic or the reasonableness of their expectations—will result in creative progress. Writers are persons who write; swimmers are (and from teaching a child I know how hard it is to persuade a reasonable person of this)—swimmers are persons who relax in the water, let their heads go down, and reach out with ease and confidence.

To strengthen my case—or to reveal its weakness—let me present two considerations. The first is example—a simple, natural procedure in writing; and the second is a considering of how even the most simple, natural construction balloons into complexity when viewed in our usual way of analyzing a piece of literature. My aim is to show that the writing is simple, if it is done by the swimming-in-itself technique; but that in analyzing the writing we can make it appear almost impossibly difficult.

First—the simple piece of writing. Doodling around one morning, I found myself with the aimless clause "While she was talking." This set of words led me to add to it, by a natural dog-paddling impulse, a closure for the construction; I wanted to have something be happening—just anything. I put down "a bear happened

along." I remembered the bears we had seen at Banff—
swaggering bears, dangerous and advertised as such, but
valued. They were violent, or potentially so; they were
protected by law. I began to put together phrases from
that trip to Banff, from that set of impressions; the re-
sult was a poem. Here it is—the simple, even poverty-
stricken phrasing of it. Where I could not think of any-
thing new to say, I repeated:

The Woman at Banff

While she was talking a bear happened along, violating
every garbage can. Shaking its loose, Churchillian,
V for victory suit, it ripped up and ate
a greasy "Bears Are Dangerous" sign.

While she was talking the trees above signalled—
"Few," and the rock back of them—"Cold."
And while she was talking a moose—huge, black—
swam that river and faded off winterward,

Up toward the Saskatchewan.

When I look at this, it appears to move inevitably;
and I see that my failure of invention—about describing
the woman—has turned into the main invention; she has
become demonstrably talkative. Turning from further
enticements—say, the rich offering of syllables in "Sas-
katchewan"—I cite one other short sample, a form so
elementary that I hardly know how to apologize enough
for it. One morning, doodling, trying to write before I
could think, I put down, "The seed that met water. . . ."
Of course, this kind of meeting is potential, in a small
way, and my next move was to crawfish back from that
potential, even while allowing it to exist, by saying that
the seed that met water "spoke a little name." By this

time I was in retreat, and I give you the poem, mostly just a little evasion, or excursion, then a payoff.

B.C.

The seed that met water spoke a little name.

(Great sunflowers were lording the air that day;
this was before Jesus, before Rome; that other air
was readying our hundreds of years to say things
that rain has beat down on over broken stones
and heaped behind us in many slag lands.)

Quiet in the earth a drop of water came,
and the little seed spoke: "Sequoia is my name."

Shrugging off a hunch that my own writing may be too disquietingly relevant to this point about simplicity, I turn to my second of the converging points—how complex the writing can be when viewed from outside, when analyzed. If a person looks at a group of words he can find ideas, sound patterns, all kinds of involuted accomplishments. They are there; human beings are so marvelous in their thinking and in their analyzing that there is no end to the complexity of what can be discovered. This complexity is our opportunity and our triumph: it is not at all my intention to belittle either the existence of or the discovery of these complexities. My point is a slightly different one. I want to plead for the ease of finding and expressing these patterns, these accomplishments which come naturally to the mind. I propose that we start with the assumption that people, even the "shallowest," do have ideas; ideas spring from motion, and the mind is always in motion. Just as the swimmer does not have a succession of handholds hidden in the water, but instead simply sweeps that yielding medium and finds it hurrying him along, so the writer passes his attention through what is at hand, and is propelled by a medium too thin and all-pervasive for the perceptions of nonbelievers who try to stay on the bank and fathom his accomplishment.

Take some aspect of technique as an example. For a nonswimmer—a nonwriter, I mean—it might seem that part of the effort of forming a poem derives from having to locate certain reinforcing sounds; to be firm about this, let us assume that the sounds needed are rhyme sounds. Maybe the writer is to move along—duh-dah, duh-dah, duh-dah, June; duh-dah, duh-dah, duh-dah, Moon. Attention becomes focused on the rhymes. Writing, however, depends to a large extent on a kind of attention the opposite of that alerted by rhyme-search. Maybe it would help to assume something like this: for the writer (prose or poetry) all words rhyme, sort of; that is, all sounded words are more like each other than any word is like silence. You start from an assumption of relation, and your experience with the language is a continuous experience with more or less similar sounds. You are always modulating along in sound. The writer and the speaker always live in one big chime. And of course this felt relation to the language consists of more than just sound-relations: syllables, aside from their sound, just in their associations in other words, have character, have cousins, enemies, checker patterns, figure-eight twists; and larger units have implications beyond their literal statements: 2 plus 2 equals 4 becomes a political statement—I believe it is still a Republican statement, though I may be missing some new developments these days. Anyway, the writer works from close similarities; he is buoyed by millions of slight influences. No analysis is ever complex enough to exhaust the potential in the language of any writer, of any human being; but on the other hand no act of writing when considered from the inside is ever anything but natural, for the writer, the person who writes, who is led by the end of whatever golden string he happens to pick up, and sustained by the self—his own appreciative self—which judges him.

To glimpse how much more pervasive than simple rhyme are the influences which come to bear in an actual passage, consider the writing potentials, neither rhyme nor not rhyme, in something Milton wrote when he herded the language ahead of him, saying and biting at once: "Avenge, O Lord, Thy slaughtered saints, whose bones/Lie scattered. . . ."

A person writes by means of that meager but persistent little self he has with him all the time. He does not outflank his ignorance by intensive reading in composition class; he does not become brilliant about constructions by learning the history of the language. He is a certain weight of person, relying on the total feeling he has for experience. Consider some implications in writing and in interchanging about it; for instance, a student brings something to discuss, saying, "I don't know whether this is really good, or whether I should throw it in the wastebasket." The assumption is that one or the other choice is the right move. No. Almost everything we say or think or do—or write—comes in that spacious human area bounded by something this side of the sublime and something above the unforgivable. We must accustom ourselves to talking without orating, and to writing without achieving "Paradise Lost." We must forgive ourselves and each other much, in our writing and in our talking. We must abjure the "I wrote it last night and it looked good, but today I see it is terrible" stance. When you write, simply tell me something. Maybe you can tell me how we should live.

For Kit, it was easy—she knew; and I can receive again the content, the pattern, the beginnings of a wonderful turbulence in her little dog-paddling toward great expression, as the two of us kept awake that night, coming through the Coast Range:

> We'd have a old car, the kind that gets
> flat tires, but inside would be wolfskin. . . .

Capturing "People of the South Wind"

Thoughts, statements, implications, are much more various, unaccountable, and free flowing than most intentional people would lead us to assume. The appearance, or the sound, or the whole feel, of the world can be changed at will. Set free, the mind discovers shortcuts and arabesques through and over and around all purposes.

Now—what would happen if you ventured into a sequence of these arabesques and shortcuts, straying from conscious intention but staying true to the immediate *feel* of what is happening? Would a pattern emerge? Yes, it would. Do you have to be careful to make a meaningful pattern emerge? No. And could that pattern that naturally emerges become a poem? Of course.

Instead of presenting such a poem and then explaining it, I would like to present some speculations and impulses and from them climb outward farther and farther toward one of the possible poems where these impulses begin to vibrate right, out there at what I could call their "periphery of justice." So—suppose a landscape that hints at the presence of people you do not meet. They could be quiet, withdrawn, infinitely wise. I imagine such people, and call them "People of the South Wind," after a tribe that used to live on the prairies. Now, these people would inhabit a world in which natural events could come about in terms of a big story behind everything. Maybe the sun, for instance, is staring around because it is hunting something. I can imagine a statement about such a scene: "One day Sun found a new canyon"—and then I let my speculations link forward from that one assertion based on the presumed lives of an extraordinary people. Whether I really believe my hunch or tentative pattern is not the point. I enter the sequence, turn the world a little to one side, and then discover the results of a sustained sequence, adventuring along into a developing pattern that grows from accepting opportunities that come along, not from following a plan or a conviction.

Here's the poem—a periphery of justice—that resulted from this kind of adventure into the crystalizing potential of a people, the people of the south wind:

1

One day Sun found a new canyon.
It hid for miles and ran far away,
then it went under a mountain. Now Sun
goes over but knows it is there. And that
is why Sun shines—it is always looking.
Be like the sun.

2

Your breath has a little shape—
you can see it cold days. Well,
every day it is like that, even in summer.
Well, your breath goes, a whole
army of little shapes. They are living
in the woods now and are your friends.
When you die—well, you go with
your last breath and find the others.

And in open places in the woods
all of you are together and happy.

3

Sometimes if a man is evil his breath
runs away and hides from him. When he
dies his last breath cannot find the others,
and he never comes together again—
those little breaths, you know, in the autumn
they scurry the bushes before the snow.
They never come back.

4

You know where the main river runs—well, for
five days below is No One, and out in the desert
on each side his children live.
They have their tents that echo dust
and give a call for their father
when you knock for acquaintance:
"No One, No One, No One."

When you cross that land the sandbars
have his name in little tracks
the mice inscribe under the bushes,
and on pools you read his wide, bland
reply to all that you ask. You wake
from dreams and hear the end of things:
"No One, No One, No One."

So much for my poem. It is possible for me to
dismantle the lines and reduce them to patterns of
apparently rigged opportunities. For example, it might
occur to me to have an extreme line: "No One, No One,
No One." Then why not build a setting to justify
such a line? Or it might be fun to assert something

outrageous and then give yourself and your audience a jab of sudden justification—not an adequate justification perhaps, but the quick excitement of a beginning belief. For example, this: "Your breath has a little shape—you can see it cold days." It might be fun to smuggle many cousin sounds so closely together that a reader would miss recognitions but still be influenced—for example, this: "One day Sun found a new canyon." It might be fun to sequence along with the reader and then shift perspective and make an extreme demand—for example, this: "Be like the sun."

It might even be fun to stumble along through wording that would ordinarily be considered awkward, but make that very awkwardness be itself a part of the effect—for example, this: "Well, every day it is like that, even in summer. Well, your breath goes. . . ." These extra syllables—"well . . . well . . . well"—that would ordinarily be cluttering up the talk could become some kind of meaningful part of the sequence.

If you have indulged me through this pattern of speculation, you have become like those people of the south wind, and have experienced a wild visioning. I now ask you to accept something even wilder. Someone asks you how you write a poem, and you begin to explain. You send forth many speculations and reasons; you watch them go. No matter how fast and how far they go, it is never enough. They never catch the actual poem, and they never come back. . . .

You see, if I try to witness adequately about how it feels to enter the creative trance, I have to put quite a test on ordinary explanations, the kind of explaining we can do when we are doing the usual planning, assembling of parts, arriving at an objective, and then assessing how well we have accomplished what we set out to do. I want, instead of that usual way of explaining things, to make a clear witness for a wilder, unplanned, utterly trustworthy process. I'll try several blunt statements about that process, always realizing that it is too odd for neat formulation.

First—intention endangers creation. True, intention seems to work well in some kinds of projects, where we want to prevail in a hurry, where we are competing. But I want to raise the question of whether creation isn't something other than putting together materials into the service of a preselected goal. Hence—intention endangers creation.

Second—let me worry around that "periphery of justice" phrasing. It's like this: how you feel can lead to a closure not related to any other end than its own satisfaction. I'm not sure the phrasing is helpful, but "periphery of justice" is my groping attempt to establish some kind of terminology for that feeling you have when you go along accepting what occurs to you and finding your way out somewhere to the rim where you are ready to abandon that sequence and come back and start all over again.

Third—when I said that I would go back and dismantle the lines of my poem, it might sound as if I were discrediting what the lines said. No, I feel that I was somehow affirming those lines, discovering their real, internal source. What might sound like reducing the importance of the language in which something is said—this could really be just discovering something about the feeling in a statement, what validates it for both speaker and hearer. The dance of syllables in "One day Sun found a new canyon" is part of what makes it stick.

The spirit back of all I've said is this: an intentional person is too effective to be a good guide in the tentative activity of creating. I think it takes a certain amount of irresponsibility, to create. And now I find a paradox in my present role. I'm supposed to be responsible in what I am saying, and of course in a way I *am* being responsible. But I'm being responsible in a pretty reckless way, because this is an odd activity, creating.

The End of a Golden String

My mother would say abrupt things, reckless things, liberating things. I remember her saying of some people in town, "They are so boring you get tired of them, even when they are not around." My children say very odd things. Their conversations, collected into a book I cherish called "Lost Words," can entertain. I came across a recent example, saved in notes from the old days. Two little ones were pretending a telephone conversation:

"How are your children?"

"They're dead."

"Chicken pox?"

"No, the hear-ache."

These are just samples recollected. I could recall for hours. But the intent is to identify only, to snag one little point: what people say—the people around us—floods our attention and then passes; it alerts us, now and then jiggles our feelings or provides a sigh or a laugh, or a combination. "How are your children?" "They're dead." We can make these passing phrases recur, change their context, add a new, immediate feeling—and resonate with unexpected force. The everyday talk around us throbs waxing and waning interest and possibility.

I want to come back to this one little snagged point.

Sometimes a person says to a writer, "What great writer most influenced you?" It is an engaging question. It almost always elicits a search for favorite authors, for passages to recall with satisfaction. Many of my friends can detect in themselves traces of pure gold—Hardy, Tennyson, Joyce, even veins of George Eliot or Shakespeare. Some find current swagger—in Mailer, or Carrie Jacobs Bond. The search for influence has appeal, as we can easily see. I would not want to spoil the fun.

Further, not just the living embodiments of former greatness take pleasure in this tracing of influences. Critics live by it. And teachers mix it with other ingredients to provide stretch and keeping qualities to the long, spinning spiel that serves them through class time and earns the daily bread. When I was in graduate school I was finely trained in this detection. For a spell of several weeks just before the ultimate pressure of my orals, I could group selected writers into their segmented, linear schools—puritan strains of the later seventeenth century, pre-Romantics sniffing toward Wordsworth. Less for boasting than for identifying, I would classify myself still as one able to slot pretty well through the whole College Outline Series.

To identify neutrally this impulse almost universal amongst scholars and teachers is to hint some questioning of it. But of course writers are influenced by earlier writers. Of course there are schools and trends in the arts. Of course in education we dwell on the achievements of those who have gone before. Surely no one could seriously question the system that has served so long and been used, explicitly and implicitly, by our whole culture, in the schools. Of course, and surely. But. I do want to give the relay-race assumption in the arts a thump. It has served, and it still serves. It lends itself to sustained scholarship. It is a life preserver for teachers on the long float through the afternoon. But the relay-race assumption distorts.

Admittedly, this issue is imposing. Writers have almost always witnessed about their reliance on models. Writers read each other, and imitate, and blend, and react to traditions in literature. Teachers—and the most imposing and successful of teachers—trace with their students the residues of earlier writers in the achievements of later ones. The subtlety and reach and eloquence in these weavings and recognitions must impress those of us who learn in the tradition. We have all experienced the search and discovery, the classifying and evaluating in terms of influences.

If you think about how flourishing and convenient the whole pattern of sequential influence is, in practicing and assessing the arts, you can see why I hesitate to make my turn and give the thump implied by my careful approach. Further, I am in danger of seeming to attack more or less than I intend. Here is the charge, and the limit on the charge, that I want to bring: the accumulated results, the convenience, and the wide acceptance of literary scholarship as a way of approaching individual works create a hazard for all who would understand how art, the doing of it, comes about. Literary scholarship, because of its convenience and success, calls for special caution on the part of teachers and students.

Let me try to untangle my charge, starting with the actual feel of writing a new thing, something never before formulated. By an easy gradient, I imagine a writer in the first degree of momentum on a new work. All directions are out from the center, the condition of stillness. A state of feeling, immediate surroundings, closest companions, whatever begins to occur to the writer—all the influences, stretching back through daily life, into early experiences, past family talk, with a mother's encouragement or criticism—all of these pieces hover for the next move. Out of all these pieces, some—for a writer—will be literary. To choose an extreme, maybe the writer puts down on paper what begins to be a sonnet. The most easily identified characteristics of the product will be literary, and the simplest, most mechanical elements will be the most easily identified. But the motivations, the pervasive influences, the distinctive elements that mark the writing will be available only to those who fall into the page as if into a strange land.

Elements easiest to identify and talk about are ones recurrent from other pieces of literature, but those recurrences are not the motivation or distinction or most significant parts of the work. The writer, even if induced by custom or laziness to do so, should not characterize his effort by predominant reference to other literary works. Each move grows out of resonance between an individual's situation and the emerging effects at the time of composition. Literature is not like a relay race, with a changing baton passed from person to person, but like something more horizontal and immediate, something that develops amid influences that for the most part are not literary.

It is easy to assume that any poem grew from another poem, but a regress into remote time, attributing each present to a literary past, ultimately runs out into some kind of present in which a person and a world encountered each other and sparked something not dependent on formulations but on involvement with material in an encounter from which original things grew. For a writer, that one-to-one encounter with materials is much more important than having a place in a sequence of writers.

Think of a person centered in a life and ready to follow leads into creating something. It might seem that such a person would need education, wide experience, and coaching in order to achieve anything impressive and intense in the arts. But any such person, no matter how remote, uneducated, and tranquil, is caught up in one, long cliff-hanger novel of a life which we might title "Inhale, Exhale": at any minute the experience of living can alternate from security to the most intense and dangerous of deprivations based on nothing more unusual than breathing. Viewed in this way, the artist is not so much a person endowed with the luck of vivid, eventful days, as a person for whom any immediate encounter leads by little degrees to the implications always present for anyone anywhere. A tradition may appear to an outsider as being crucially involved, but the "tradition" derives from sense encountering related elements, not from an intellect relating to a pattern.

I will descend all the way to a particular, to a poem, this one called "The Trip":

> Our car was fierce enough;
> no one could tell we were only ourselves;
> so we drove, equals of the car,
> and ate at a drive-in where Citizens were dining.
> A waitress with eyes made up to be Eyes
> brought food spiced by the neon light.
>
> Watching, we saw the manager greet people—
> hollow on the outside, some kind of solid veneer.
> When we got back on the road we welcomed
> it as a fierce thing welcomes the cold.
> Some people you meet are so dull
> that you always remember their names.*

*From *Traveling Through the Dark*, Harper and Row. Copyright 1962 by William Stafford.

The nearest to a tradition that I can discover for myself in this poem is in the last two lines, where I hear my mother's voice again, in a remark something like the one about people so boring you get tired of them even when they are not around. But that literary influence I can claim is not all honorific. It does not come from emulation of a recognized model, but from helpless involvement in the mean feelings of a person so much like me that my style is my plight as a human being. And my poem is like a series of bumps into sensations I have under certain conditions in current life. If a scholar should tell me that my poem is a resultant from a tradition in satire, or a variation on so and so's reaction to the age of the automobile, I might plume myself on having a part in culture; but what the poem feels like is this—it feels like an extension of family gossip into trenchant statements to be made to people listening with a little more care than usual.

Now it may seem to you that in attacking the relay-race theory of literary production I am doing a minuet in an area not important to us. Maybe this concern of mine is trivial, but even a slight misplacing of emphasis might lead to big trouble, over the years, as we accept stances that give us little leverage with people who discover themselves prevalently involved in contemporary affairs and not coercively interested in establishing a theoretical relation to the past or to the accomplishments of persons whose lives apparently had little justification except as models for programmed citizens. Somewhere, each life has its validation, not in a sequence of ciphers influencing each other down through time, but in immediate encounters that have their own individual worths, no matter how small. If this contention of mine lacks force, perhaps an example will help.

In traveling to lecture I have been asked often to train my remarks around some topic like "The Influence of

T. S. Eliot on Current American Poetry." This topic I can recognize. I like to be able to relate my reading of T. S. Eliot to what I find happening now. It is even true that in my conduct on formal occasions I may find myself either being or refusing to be J. Alfred Prufrock; and I think that being—but especially refusing to be— J. Alfred Prufrock is an interesting maneuver amidst the values and lack of values around us. But in some strange way I feel that the influence of T. S. Eliot is more on other people than on current American poets. I see critics like markers in a channel, tugged by what they measure, but I see writers like minnows disporting themselves in flurries of action that avoid the current.

So it interests me that after a lecture on the influence of T. S. Eliot, many people, and especially young people, will often come up for a few remarks eddying around some such question as "What Is Really Happening?" "What Are American Poets Doing These Days?" And such questions as these bring me to the point of trying to reformulate the literary scene in such a way as to bring out a crucial difference between our way of feeling and earlier ways. Instead of tagging our time by means of adjustments in the usual ways of tracing literary influences from generation to generation, I would hazard something like this:

> Writers today in America are finding their way forward on the page by means of opportunities that occur to them as they use the language of the rest of life in conditions that invite sequential discoveries that validate themselves in terms of immediate feelings. No test of tradition is needed. No approximation to established form. No assessment as to congruence of the now experience with given or established experience.

A poem today is anything said in such a way or put on the page in such a way as to invite from the hearer or reader a certain kind of attention. Form or content will be validated by the writer's feelings and by the convergent feelings of readers, who will be caught up in the common language. Any suggestion that the language is depending on conventions established for purely "literary" experiences will be disquieting, not because such conventions were always disquieting, but because now we assume more than ever before that a convention is not a rule that makes legitimate a practice, but a temporary and changing statement of something we continue to discover: what appeals in practice establishes a basis for temporary formulations that can be called "rules," until a new discovery or feeling suggests a change, at which time not the feeling but the rule must give.

To assert a break with tradition, with certain conventions, with certain rules, is not to assert a break with order of some kind. What implications for writers, teachers, and students grow from the view asserted here? If the relay-race concept is downgraded, where do we turn? The turn toward a positive looms as troublesome, and no claim can be made for the adequacy of what follows, but here are suggestions for teachers ready to accept some opening moves. I will word the suggestions in terms of poetry, but I believe other forms of literature will yield to this approach.

My guide into open forms is suggested by my title, a quotation from William Blake's *Jerusalem*:

> I give you the end of a golden string,
> Only wind it into a ball,
> It will lead you in at Heaven's gate
> Built in Jerusalem's wall.

Writing or reading, a poem goes by sequential parts, accumulating its effect (or frittering it away) by its internal trends. Starting with anything, the pattern begins;

the little thread leads onward. If the writer is masterful and ambitious, the string may very well break; and the result may be a document on a well-chosen topic, but it will not be a developed poem. If the reader is masterful and ambitious, the interpretation may be eloquent, but if it commands the materials on the page it may very well distort and impose rather than discover. If the writer knows the market and deliberately hits a trend, the result may be a negotiable piece of work—he may get it published—but it will lose that golden string of its internal consistency, and the result will not be an increment in art, but just a marketable product. If the reader knows literary history and traditions, and forces the poem into conformity, the interpretation may link the poem to some discoverable pattern, but only at the cost of neglecting some of what is individual in the poem.

The stance to take, reading or writing, is neutral, ready, susceptible to now; such a stance is contrary to anything tense or determined or "well-trained." Only the golden string knows where it is going, and the role for a writer or reader is one of following, not imposing.

Retreating into the snug little weaving shed of the writer, I would advance, timidly, an idea contrary to the scholarly, the masterful, the eloquent. Sometimes it seems to me that a writer habitually touches the earth, touches home, clings to all that passes. Even to start a poem is to unreel stingily from the starting place, and to make each successive move out of minimum psychic expenditure. Here is something that leads like a little thread. It is called "At the Playground":

> Away down deep and away up high
> a swing drops you into the sky.
> Forth it swings you in a sweep
> all the way to the stars and back—
> Goodby, Jill, goodby, Jack.

> Shuddering climb wild and steep,
> away up high, away down deep.

Let me say that a poem comes from a life, not a study. The influences pounce upon a writer, and any rules or traditions get buffeted. Entering the sequence—writing or reading—is entering what unfolds. It is easy to talk about a tradition. It is easy to adopt a concept or metaphor (my golden string is one). Sometimes it is enticing to speak about the danger of playing tennis with the net down, if you want to claim some rules. But for the writer each poem has its own net. The essential is some kind of lead, and then a willingness to allow the development. If I start telling a poem, and try to be alert about its connections, I find internal resonances rather than traditions of literature. Something of the tonality of my mother's voice, referred to at the beginning, recurs to me now; and I feel the bite of her disappointment in life, and a wry angle of her vision. My dashing brother getting out into the big world—he recurs to me—and my father taking me out for a ride in a racing car—right down by the big engine I crouched, while Martin Shamosko revved it out North Main. And the horizontal flood gets busy in something like "Fifteen":

> South of the bridge on Seventeenth
> I found back of the willows one summer
> day a motorcycle with engine running
> as it lay on its side, ticking over
> slowly in the high grass. I was fifteen.
>
> I admired all that pulsing gleam, the
> shiny flanks, the demure headlights
> fringed where it lay; I led it gently
> to the road and stood with that
> companion, ready and friendly. I was fifteen.
>
> We could find the end of a road, meet

the sky on out Seventeenth. I thought about
hills, and patting the handle got back a
confident opinion. On the bridge we indulged
a forward feeling, a tremble. I was fifteen.

Thinking, back farther in the grass I found
the owner, just coming to, where he had flipped
over the rail. He had blood on his hand, was pale—
I helped him to his machine. He ran his hand
over it, called me good man, roared away.

I stood there, fifteen.

From this indulgence in young feelings, I want to step
back, here at the end of my witnessing about the pri-
macy of feeling and immediate reference. For my final
bid I offer what claims to be a poem and also a lecture,
even a scholarly lecture. For this last piece I beg your
friendship and indulgence, as I attempt "A Lecture on
the Elegy":

An elegy is really about the wilting of a flower,
the passing of the year, the falling of a stone.
Those people who go out, they just accompany
many things that leave us. Death is only
bad because it is like sunset, or a long eclipse.
If it had a dawn for company, or came with
spring, we would need laws to keep eager people
from rushing into danger and thus depopulating the world.

So, I have turned the occasion for such sadness
around: those graceful images that
seem to decorate the poems, they are
a rediscovery of those elements
that first created the obvious feelings,
the feelings that some people cannot even sense
until they are built up from little losses
and surrounded with labels: "war," "catastrophe," "death."*

---

*From *The Southern Review*, Winter, 1973. Copyright 1973 by
The Louisiana State University.

Writing

The Discovery of Daily Experience

It is a whisper. You turn somewhere,
hall, street, some great event: the stars
or the lights hold; your next step waits you
and the firm world waits—but
there is a whisper. You always live so,
a being that receives, or partly receives, or
fails to receive each moment's touch.

You see the people around you—the honors
they bear—a crutch, a cane, eye patch,
or the subtler ones, that fixed look, a turn
aside, or even the brave bearing: all declare
our kind, who serve on the human front and earn
whatever disguise will take them home. (I saw
Frank last week with his *crutch de guerre*.)

When the world is like this—and it is—
whispers, honors or penalties disguised—no wonder
art thrives like a pulse wherever civilized people,
or any people, live long enough in a place to
build, and remember, and anticipate; for we are
such beings as interact elaborately with what
surrounds us. The limited actual world we successively
overcome by fictions and by the mind's inventions
that cannot be quite arbitrary (and hence do reflect
the actual), but can escape the actual (and hence
may become art).

This attitude toward the immediate experience of the world may indicate why in planning to consider writing I reminded myself to be alert, to be aware of the now-ness of things—the feel of the day, the temperature, the kind of room, the people, what they said. This attempt to be aware springs from an opinion, a fear, maybe a superstition about art: any time we adopt a stance that induces an analytical feeling, we may be subverting what art depends on. Some questions may clarify this superstition of mine, and maybe the turning, swerving manner of proceeding will hint, too, at my plight amid complex issues.

Is art in things we separate for contemplation, or is it somewhere else, maybe in the attitude we adopt, the way we receive things in order to sustain a special quality of experience? If we identify certain people as "artists" and yield them the portion of life that governs the *feeling* aspect of existence, have we done right? Is the care of artists the direct way to promote art? Is the accumulation of art objects centrally important for the art activity in an area?

I will take a stand on these issues, and hope that the stand will lead to further consideration.

Art is not essentially in things we separate for con-templation or admiration. Identifying some as "artists" endangers art. The care of artists is not central to the care of art. The accumulation of art objects is peripheral to the activity of art, in any area.

Let me grope into a series of formulations, not intended to be sequential-cumulative, but intended to identify as carefully as possible the attitude this one practitioner has found most helpful in his own kind of art activity—writing. I will number the formulations.

1. The state of our give-and-take lives, the general

liveliness and bounce of our reactions—not the absolute accomplishment of a few people—is the centrally important factor in the art of our area.

2. Not a few, but everyone, makes art. There is no art beyond the sensibility of the people confronting it: art is an interaction between object and beholder. The idea of a human being forced to concede the superiority of a work of art without in fact being able to participate in judging that quality is a surrealistic idea.

3. In my area, the coyotes are still the best poets.

4. One doesn't learn how to do art, but one learns that it is possible by a certain adjustment of consciousness to participate in art—it's a natural activity for one not corrupted by mechanical ways.

5. When someone asks, "When did you start to write?" there is no way to respond adequately and briefly: for the question starts with a wrong assumption. Poetry, for instance, is not something that one takes up and begins to do; it is something that everyone is caught up in, early, and a few keep on doing.

6. Practical people assume that creating in art takes place in a mechanical manner. For example, some complex form in poetry—say, a sonnet—is analyzed. A person studies and learns that sonnets are fourteen lines long; so he counts down fourteen when he writes one. And he learns that a sonnet has five stresses in each line; so he counts five across. And he may go on to learn intricacies—a sonnet breaks between lines eight and nine; so he chops his poem decisively in that place, amid the fourteen lines. Then, putting together the successive moves he has learned, he writes a sonnet. No.

To try for another conception of how the process works, I ask that we imagine this—the first person in the world who ever wrote a sonnet. He could not learn how, by the method detailed; for of course there were no models. How did he do it? It is that other way that we are pursuing now.

7. That other way is hinted in a passage from Blake (in *Jerusalem*, the part "To the Christians"):

> I give you the end of a golden string,
>   Only wind it into a ball,
> It will lead you in at Heaven's gate
>   Built in Jerusalem's wall.

8. In art, one at a time, experiences contribute their immediate, felt existence: one reads a house, a scene, a room, a space, a sequence, etc. In writing, for instance, the quality of the work and its effects on the feelings are .welcomed at once. One does the documentary of what is happening—the whole orchestration including the personal reaction—while the activity is happening. The feel of our lives, instead of being disregarded or slighted, is accepted as important.

Any little impulse is accepted, and enhanced. A person writing may feel, for instance, that at the end of a line he is using up that little space for a break in his sentence that would be a break even if the end of the line did not come at that point: he may decide to break the line at some point where he can gain a slight bonus that would not be there if he did not end the line at that point.

9. The inner-validation aspect of art may be suggested by spelling out the attitude of a reader of literature. Here is my way: I read and keep on reading as a resultant of motivations—if I go on, it is by a *net* impulse to go forward. That net impulse may derive partly from mere promise—if there is reason to believe that ultimate reward awaits, even if current feeling is negative, I will enter into a deficit relation with an unliked

text, a currently unrewarding sequence. But lacking such promise—and even with such promise in the case of a novel, story, or poem—I read only by congenial motivation. If I have to push the story, read from duty, I let it go. If the text displeases me, or just keeps on promising me later good by *saying*, not demonstrating, I let it go. My resultant formulation from this process: creative writing is that kind of communication that lives by its immediate authority as appealing to the sensibilities of a reader.

10. The inner-validation aspect of literature may be turned around, by considering how it feels to write something—how the process works without depending on a pattern or rule. It seems that all experiences of a certain tonality or flavor vibrate together when a new experience of that tonality or flavor happens or is referred to or elicited in any way. Why do I say "certain tonality or flavor"—such a vague phrasing? Because that congeniality is not to be identified by more precise designations, not by intention, or worldly result, but by feeling. And one therefore cannot plan to elicit that result; one must find it by willingly entering an area of possible encounter. The immediacy of each encounter is the guide for the sequential moves. To have in mind patterns other than those dictated by immediate experience is to violate the process you must depend on. It is the prior election, and consequently the neglect of actual experience, that stultifies the work of artists who propagandize, for instance: they have taken a line of progression that tries to validate itself by preelected reference points. Such writers get lost.

11. By contrast to the writer who preselects his objectives, one can speculate about the art-bonuses available to those who enter freely into the process. At an extreme, one could claim a great deal. When you

enter art, you may be allowing a self you have only partly, to enjoy its best choices. The action of writing, for instance, is the successive discovery of cumulative epiphanies in the self's encounter with the world. It would be too much to claim that art, the practice of it, will establish a "good," a serene, a superior self. No. But art will, if pursued for itself and not for adventitious reasons or by spurious ways, bring into sustained realization the self most centrally yours, freed from its distortions brought from greed, or fear, or ambition.

Art has its sacramental aspect. The source of art's power is one with religion's: the discovery of the essential self and the cultivation of it through the act of its positive impulses.

This turning to the inward self is especially important in our time, when literature is merchandised. *Time, Newsweek*, talk shows, and many such "guides" to our opinions, give us a package. They identify literature in the careless, brush-by way we all accept when we accept the intentional, commercial pattern for everyday life. We do not perceive that our language and our purpose-oriented habits are making us violate again and again the distinction that this inner, art, activity has. The "important" institutions of our time judge literature by the prevalent clichés of our time; but literature springs us out of time.

The Practice of Composing in Language

Composing in language is done by feel, rather than by rule. Yes, many critics, and many writers too, will discuss the process and often settle for statements that identify pattern results; but back of summary statements there hovers a whole ocean of tentatives in the consciousness of the writer.

Anything we say or anything we write comes to us sequentially with a host of moving, bobbing opportunities. The practice of writing involves a readiness to accept what emerges, what entices. The sound of words and phrases, the associations of those sounds and syllables in words, the emerging trajectory of thought and feeling, that background of conditioning wrought by earlier writers, the individual bite, or whine, or snarl, or whatever, of the local family dialect—all of these and no doubt many others—influence the results. A writer coasts into action with willing involvement, always ready for something to happen that may be a first time, not a repetition of something already accomplished.

Ready for adventure, the writer waits, in the presence of the impending language: many things happen. The encounter with the language is too individual to be

From *Agenda*.

typed, helpfully, as "English" or "American"—the writer's own voice, the voice of his family, the voice of the neighborhood—those successively larger areas of relation bear on the feeling at the moment of composition; but large influences, national tendencies, or tendencies of a period in literature have much less significance than do close, local nudges from day-to-day life. Rhythm of speech will suggest enhancements of rhythm; some degree of symmetry—or pleasing asymmetry—will influence how the words go on the page. Each line will be a venturing forward from the left margin toward the right, with options for breaks or for continuity contending for recognition. The farther toward the right margin the line gets, the more crucial the passing of each option—and the length of proximate lines will also be influencing the writer.

Placement—the end of a line, for instance—makes a difference, but sometimes the difference is small; even if no pause, or little pause, occurs, the forward feeling of the poem will sustain a syncopation. Similarly, the close of a verse paragraph or stanza will invite its own cluster of options—definite closing, hovering motion leading to the next stanza, or possibly even a felt leap without a pause. But even to violate a usual pause is one kind of experience. The writer will be working in the presence of all sound effects. There is no escape from such effects, in either direction—toward a pattern that appears to limit choices, or away from a pattern that seems to neglect sounds. They are there; they make a difference.

But to live your writing life by assuming that certain "norms" have been established and thereby made operative for any writer—such a stance reverses the actual: writers recognize opportunities; if a group or a tradition recognizes certain opportunities and makes that recognition into a "norm," the range of options is not changed. Anyone may come along and move into composing the language by means of hints and hunches that occur to an individual. All of our friends have norms and other habits; but the part of an artist is to make any present action the occasion for emergence from present potentials. Norms are for talking about art; opportunities are for artists. And back of any "norm" is speech; how talk goes will live—whether neglected by intent or not.

Any break at a line, any caesura, any surfacing of natural syllable intonation—these are all a total of language-feel that the writer orchestrates according to what comes along in the act of composing. There is no syncopation impossible; the total effect in the experience of the writer at the moment is totally in command.

So, everything makes a difference: a word at the end or beginning of a line is different from a word elsewhere in the line; any syllable that customarily gets slurred in speech carries at least the ghost of that slurring into the most formal context; any emergency in the throat is an event in the poem. To change anything—the length of a line, the sequence of pronunciation of syllables by reversing words—anything—will influence the feel of the language.

In such an ocean of mutual influences, the trajectory of acceptance for certain practices—pentameter, the vogue of it, for instance—will vary in steepness and significance. Pentameter will not come or go away just at the whim of a writer, who may do lines by fives or not by fives, but continues to engage with readers who will put the pentameter overlay onto anything heard, or will shy from that overlay. And rhyme—no one can escape similar sounds, or make hearers accept patterns beyond their hearing readiness. One who composes in language moves in the presence of sound, more or less similar sounds; moves in the presence of speech sequences; breathes with a set of muscles that will clutter or enhance the ever-varying physical presence of language effects.

One who composes in language confronts opportunity too varied for fixed rules, or for violation of rules: from the emergency of the encounter emerges the new realization, the now poem.

Some Arguments Against Good Diction

. . . it is with words mainly that we delineate the conceivable and if we never allow words to be a little eccentric, never allow ourselves to apply a word to any state of affairs actual or conceivable, to which it would not customarily be applied, we are without means to refer to any state of affairs for which there is not a word, any possibility undreamt of in our philosophy.*

Ordinary statements about diction and literature and the process of writing often have such convenience and such easy links to what we say about other activities, that we are tempted to accept the superficial formula. This tendency—a kind of Gresham's law of art discussion—we have to guard against. Whatever is distinctive in some intricate activity is *felt* by the practitioners, but in talking about the activity with others (and even in conceiving it to themselves), people accept quick formulations that *generally* help. But the cumulative effect of the assumptions thus woven into art discussion becomes misleading. To avoid such misunderstandings, we try restating, but we have to use the language, again full of distortions; so we do something like taking off

*John Wisdom, *Paradox and Discovery* (Oxford: Basil Blackwell, 1965), p. 132.

a rubber glove with one hand, and it is a glove that *wants to stay on.*

One such topic confounded by Gresham's law is that of diction. Apparently for many people the writer is conceived as a person sitting at a big desk with cubbyholes containing all the words there are—or all the words the writer knows. The person writes his story or essay, or anything, by carefully reaching with long tweezers into the cubbyholes to get the right words (proper words in proper places—everyone knows that poems are made with words). *Le mot juste* is the slogan of excellence in writing.

Following the implied advice of such a picture and of those apparently helpful phrasings, a novice learns an adequate vocabulary, sits down at his desk with all the cubbyholes, and is a writer. But somehow he does not write *War and Peace.* That picture and those words have misled the would-be writer, and they can even menace the accomplished writer who lives perilously surrounded by such pleasant, simple concepts and sayings that superficially delineate his art.

The process of writing that I experience has little connection with the formulations I most often hear. Where words come from, into consciousness, baffles me. Speaking or writing, the words bounce instantaneously into their context, and I am victimized by them, rather than controlling them. They do not wait for my selection; they volunteer. True, I can reject them, but my whole way of writing induces easy acceptance—at first—of any eager volunteer. I want to talk about these volunteers, but first want to consider another reason for trying carefully to set the record straight, about attitudes toward language. The point concerns how a writer feels about language, in general. Many opine that a writer, and particularly a poet, for some reason, must love language; often there is even a worshipful attitude assumed. I have noticed this assumption with particular attention because it happens that insofar as I can assess my own attitudes in relation to others' I have an unusually intense distrust of language. What people say or write comes to me attenuated or thinned by my realization that talk merely puts into the air an audio counterpart of mysterious, untrustworthy, confused events in the creature making the sounds. "Truth," or "wonder," or any kind of imaginative counterpart of "absolute realities"—these I certainly do not expect in human communication.

An illustration of this distrust—an illustration that brings in contrary attitudes held by very imposing people, and hence is highly dangerous for my own case—came when I saw inscribed in gold on a pillar in the Library of Congress this saying: "The inquiry, knowledge and belief of truth is the sovereign good of human nature." To me, such a saying is hollow; I see it as demonstrating man's pathetic infatuation with an apparent power that is essentially just a redundancy. The highest we know is high for us, but its communication is an interior, not an absolute, phenomenon. And I cringe to realize that my own saying of my kind of truth is hazardous at best. Language—others' and my own—is very thin.

But back to diction. When we talk or write we venture into an immediate engagement with the language we happen to have. This accumulation of sounds and assumptions and automatic, unconscious logicings provides us with a progressing experience we feel as meaningful. If we find ourselves in a state of emergency when applying our natural language to the emerging opportunities, we can slog through words and make some kind of communication without necessarily feeling that the language is being helpful in any local way—we speak or write in a workaday fashion, and our language may not have any lift or "poetic" feeling. That is one way to use the language.

Another way is to let the language itself begin to shape the event taking place by its means. If it happens that at this time in history and at this place in our own experience we happen on a word with a syllable that reverberates with many other syllables in contexts that reinforce what the immediate word is doing, we have "powerful language." The internal reinforcements of the historically opportune language we happen to own come into something like focus or harmony. We speak or write poetry. Even if what we write is prose, we may speak of it as "poetical." This kind of link with poetry I take to mean that some kind of dynamism in the language itself—syllables, cadences, local or larger surges in sound or imagery—is carrying the *now*-conditioned reader or hearer into his own blissful redundancy inside his own experience. Like the philosophers who admire the scope of thought, the artists are exhilarated by the "power of art."

Let me try for a direct statement on what is disquieting about what ordinarily surfaces when we talk about "good diction." For a writer, it is not the past or present of words that counts, but their futures, and those futures are approaching by means of influences too various for rules or derivations to control or predict. When the poet says, "The fog comes pussyfooting along," or something like that, it isn't that the isolated words have been drafted, but that some kind of yearning connection among experiences has taken over. Reluctantly, the writer enters language and fearfully entrusts that limited and treacherous medium to keep from absolutely violating the feeling he has entrusted to it. In the ensuing transaction, language accomplishes several things at once.

1. It begins to distort, by congealing parts of the total experience into successive, partially relevant signals (just as this sentence is doing now).

2. It begins to entice the reader or hearer away into his own version or variation on the speaker's or writer's relations to the words.

3. But—and an important but—the transaction also begins to enhance the experience because of a weird quality in language: the successive distortions of language have their own kind of cumulative potential, and under certain conditions the distortions of language can reverberate into new experiences more various, more powerful, and more revealing than the experiences that set off language in the first place.

It is that cumulative potential in language that writers find themselves relying on again and again as they fearfully advance, leaving behind some of the purposes and aims they started with and accepting the wondrous bonuses that chance and the *realizing* elements of the future's approach allows them. *Le mot juste* does not exist. For people, the truth does not exist. But language offers a continuous encounter with our own laminated, enriched experiences; and sometimes those encounters lead to further satisfactions derived from the cumulative influences in language as it spins out. That kind of language experience we grope for and identify with various tags. One of them is just a word—poetry.

Making a Poem / Starting a Car on Ice

A poem is anything said in such a way or put on the page in such a way as to invite from the hearer or reader a certain kind of attention. The kind of attention that is invited will appear—sort of—in what follows.

This way of identifying a poem shies away from using content or form, or any neat means. It is not meter or rhyme, or any easily seen pattern, or any selected kind of content, or any contact with gods, or a goddess, that is crucial—it is some kind of signal to the receiver that what is going on will be a performance that merits an alertness about life right at the time of living it. You can even make something not a poem become a poem by looking at it a certain way, or listening to it a certain way. Found poems are this kind of experience. They are all around us, we come to suspect; and by a certain squint or a certain way of leaning our ears, we find them. (Those whose ears don't lean may feel free to shake them sadly now.)

Once at the University of Washington a student made me aware of this oddity in a poem. She brought into the office a big scroll that when unwound said something like "Please/consider others/Smoking may shorten their lives/and may deprive them/of your living presence"—something like that. Not having a good place to display this scroll, I turned back the top of the sheet and put a book on it so that the message hung along a bookcase by my desk. The writer told me that this was her poem for the day, and that our kind of people no longer accepted orders like "No Smoking," and that poetry should function as part of the information system for society. She said her scroll was a poem. Squinting, I saw it. (I always do.) Well, after she left another student came in. He settled in a chair by the desk, got out cigarettes, and prepared to light up. Then he saw the scroll. He hastily started to put his cigarettes away, but when I said, "It's a poem," he immediately went ahead and lighted up. He examined the scroll, through the smoke he was making, and admired it. Squinting again, I thought I saw something about what a poem is.

It might be possible to elaborate on that scene to draw lessons from it, but to do so might endanger the intuition that flowered there in the office that day. It is almost as if some intuitions survive only if they are not dissected.

But it may be all right to range around for some others; and taken together they may identify each other.

For instance, try this: If you compose a poem you start without any authority. If you were a scientist, if you were an explorer who had been to the moon, if you were a knowing witness about the content being presented—you could put a draft on your hearer's or reader's belief. Whatever you said would have the force of that accumulated background of information; and any mumbles, mistakes, dithering, could be forgiven as not directly related to the authority you were offering.

But a poet—whatever you are saying, and however you are saying it, the only authority you have builds from the immediate performance, or it does not build. The moon you are describing is the one you are creating. From the very beginning of your utterance you are creating your own authority.

Surely we all know that falsity in reading a poem and judging it in terms of the author's name. We know that the writer's past—though it may deserve commendation—is not to be used to validate the current work. A poem has to stand by itself, no matter how many prizes the writer has won. Further, we have suffered as readers when editors choose to publish by relying on the past work of an author. There is momentum and competition for names, but these understandable influences put a strain on the more important requirement that authority depends on current performance. The adventitious influences that get into the scene are always trying to corrupt the angel in us that relates to art.

This immediate-validation requirement is a constant excitement in writing. The distinction of the artist is this working in the presence of the recording angel at all times. Put so, the life of art sounds frightening, and many people find it that way. We know the turmoil and dishonesty and pride and jealousy, and breakdown, that flourish in competitive life under such conditions of constant responsibility. But without blinking that frightening connection between performance and merit, I have impulses to make art experiences that avoid strain, avoid competition. Come to think of it, though, this may be another intuition that wouldn't survive having its wings pulled off. Let me turn instead to an actual poem, one that came to me. Lean me your ears.

Once, in the morning, I took my writing position—lying on the couch by the front window—and looked out.

Two of our children were away at college. The house was quiet. I saw that I should weed the lawn. And with these preliminary thoughts I began to write—this:

> When the wind ended and we came down
> it was grass all around. One of us found
> the dirt—it was rich, black and easy.
> When it rained, we began to grow, except
> two of us caught in leaves and unable to touch
> earth, which always starts things. By late June
> we sent our own off, just as we had done, floating
> that wonderful wind that promises new land. Now
> spread low and flat, on this precious part of the world,
> but my dreams—where have they found? I wish
> them well

This is the way it went, as clearly as I can decipher the scribble of that morning—the page is full of revisions and words run up the page, and some additions. But that morning it was as lined out above. Later I squinted those lines, and began to see a poem there. Skipping the intervening steps, I want to give what resulted and was published. Then I want to put pressure on the whole operation, to link with earlier assertions.

Whispered into the Ground

> Where the wind ended and we came down
> it was all grass. Some of us found
> a way to the dirt—easy and rich.
> When it rained, we grew, except
> those of us caught up in leaves, not touching
> earth, which always starts things.
> Often we sent off our own
> just as we'd done, floating that
> wonderful wind that promised new land.
>
> Here now spread low, flat on this
> precious part of the world, we miss

> those dreams—and the strange old places
> we left behind. We quietly wait.
> The wind keeps telling us something
> we want to pass on to the world:
> Even far things are real.

For what it is, I want to use this poem; its weaknesses can furbish into strength, when used aright. And for its kind of utterance I want to attempt clear assertions. First—how it draws from nearby things its onward trend, becomes a found poem amid the elements that happen to be there: the lawn, the quiet house (but home), the children away at college. It makes its move to emerge as sound—ground, down, found—but turns away from relying on such patterns and relaxes into dirt, caught, own, done, and slows into land. Its beginning is traction on the ice between writer and reader— statements that do not demand much belief, easy claims, even undeniable progressions without need of authority. No solicitation of the reader's faith: come along if you like; don't expect much. If the reader or listener enters the poem, I want the moves to come from inside the poem, the coercion to be part of the life right there.

But now it is time to take better aim, to confess biases— or to reduce the proud assertions. Let me put it this way: in the past, a poet might make big initial claims. With the mantle accorded the artist, the poet prophesies:

> Avenge, O Lord, thy slaughtered saints, whose bones . . .

And even in recent times the prophetical fervor could scat-start a poem:

> I saw the best minds of my generation destroyed by madness . . .

These poems to be declaimed, are proclaimed. And many fervent voices announce themselves and make clear poems, even today. But champions now are scarce. Depletion of faith is hard to overcome. Inside the voice that makes extreme requests of us, there must be accompanying, quick validation; we must have ready proof in the lines that the author is worthy company. And even then we want to make our own judgments, from the context we share with the teller. If the voice makes extreme claims but demonstrates no quality commensurate with its demands, the poem gasps at once.

But again—this analysis begins to endanger the vagueness necessary for art. There is a distinction between workaday processes and the process that brings about poems. Writers have many things to be careful not to know—and strangely one of the things not to know is how to write. Sometimes writers who have wandered into good poems have become too adept. Auden was one. Someplace he said he feared repeating himself as the years went by, and this fear shocked me, for it undercut a view I have long cherished—that a writer is not trying for a product, but accepting sequential signals and adjustments toward an always-arriving present. To slight that readiness—even in order to avoid repetition—would be to violate the process, would be to make writing into a craft that neglected its contact with the ground of its distinction. Auden's remark sufficed for wit, but wit can blur what the poet does. And Auden's own best poems stumble into each other again and again, seeking a center that belongs there.

More congenial in its attitude toward writing is something Thomas Mann said in *A Sketch of My Life* (Knopf, 1960):

> The truth is that every piece of work is a realization, fragmentary but complete in itself, of our individuality; and this kind of realization is the sole and painful way we have of getting the particular experience—no wonder, then, that the process is attended by surprises.

Many remarks from writers give this kind of glimpse into how they actually feel when entering the activity; frequently they say something like, "It was only recently that I was able to write this poem." The implication is that writing is something other than just an intention and the craft to carry it out. Writing is a reckless encounter with whatever comes along.

There are worthy human experiences that become possible only if you accept successive, limited human commitments, and one such is the sustained life of writing. It is far from an austere, competitive, fastidious engagement with the best, as outsiders might think. A writer must write bad poems, as they come, among the better, and not scorn the "bad" ones. Finicky ways can dry up the sources. And a poem may be indictable for weaknesses, without thereby yielding itself to "correction"; there may be flaws necessary for even the faltering accomplishment embodied in the poem. To avoid the flaws might lead to one big flaw—the denying of leads that carry the writer on.

And so I have entangled myself in denying the validity of what I am doing—explaining how to start and run a poem. Well, the ice is slicker than it used to be, when the heroes gunned their motors. Actually, I like it this way. It's quieter. And for too long we have been accepting moon rocks from people who live right where we live. We all have to earn any moon we present. The only real poems are found poems—found when we stumble on things around us.

When typing out "Whispered into the Ground" cited earlier here, I began to have tremors of realization—feedback from patterns deeper even than the relation between the poem and our house, and the children away. I realized that a poem written a year ago had anticipated the arguments I was even now making:

> Where the wind ended and we came down
> it was all grass. Some of us found
> a way to the dirt, easy and rich.

A wind has ended. Some of us found a way to the dirt. It is easy and rich. It always starts things. Well, almost always.

Here are some recent poems. They were lying around the desk while these prose remarks were unfolding. These poems, I found, already illustrated points I hadn't yet thought of when I wrote them.

My Mother Looked Out in the Morning

"Announced by an ax, Daniel Boone
opened the door"—the wild ones you told,
looking out from the timid person you were!

All was hard, clear sunlight, or else
dark shadow. You never had found
the way to live either one or the other,

But you always looked out, the fence
faithful, always to extend and
mean the understanding again,

And then the inner surprises,
the result of your wonder: a miracle!—
you were you, you were you, you were you.

Reversals live now, indoors and out,
where your children carry that house
and others, and are wise. You were simple—

Your stories ran wild: "Listen, Billy—
imagine the world. Make me real. Be my child."

One of the Stories

A square of color on Rayl's Hill
was a place where we often walked—
there under a new-killed Indian brave
pioneers buried a child.

(Once the tough grass that strangles flowers
is broken, you can't hide what's buried—
a burst of color will mark that square
for years on the open prairie.)

Out there in the sun an outlaw man
driven from his tribe killed a girl
because he couldn't stand her tears
when he frightened her there on the hill.

The settlers found and surrounded the man
and the father killed him in rage.
All around the prairie lay.
And the settlers were afraid.

Fearful, at night, the parents dug,
and beneath the Indian brave
to protect their own they hid the girl
from hate that could tear up a grave.

My father showed us that special square
with many a flower twined
for the double burial, one above one,
where death was used as a blind.

"Bandits may kill but be innocent,
and children may die but sin:
no one but God sees all the way down,"
our parents told us then.

And for years our family tended that place
with fear, with wonder, with prayers,
where God had sprung the prairie flowers
from whosever grave it was.

Saying a Name

Someone the far side of Neahkhanie Mountain
pronounces the name. Clouds come over
for the autumn visit again.
Every summer we try to look away,
to leave the mountain alone. Things
we don't say begin to belong—live
as the days move, lie on the sand. The blue
sky touches far, forgotten waves.

Then someone looks up. It always happens,
as it should, for the world, and the gray comes back,
saving the deep floating tops of the trees,
and the rocks lower down, and saving the reckless
people who glance too high for so late
a time, and forget, and pronounce a name.

Run Sheep Run

Once when we hid no one ever found us.
It all changed into this kind of world—your
picture repeated wherever I turn, but
none of them you, and I can't find my way back
    into our story.

This is how it is in our town:
our house faces north, in the yard
a few relics; I stand a long time
by the gate and imagine; it is cold; it is
evening. When the stars begin, I run
away over the snow, zigzagging
as fast as I can, but wherever I turn
it is the world. It is time to give up.
Wherever the others went, this is home.

Kinds of Winter

It was a big one. We followed it over
the snow. Even if it made no mistakes, we
would have it. That's what The World means—
there are kinds of winter that you meet.
And that big one had met us, its big winter.

But there was a hill, and when we rounded
it the tracks were gone. We had used up
the daylight. The wind had come and
emptied our trail, back of us, ahead of us.
We looked at each other. Our winter had come.

This message I write in the shelter of the overturned
sled. Later someone may find us
and mail this letter to you. Let me tell you something:
it doesn't make any difference what anyone ever said,
here at the last, under the snow.

Stereopticon

This can happen. They can bring the leaves back
to the cottonwood trees, those great big rooms
where our street—as long as summer—led
to the river. From a rusty nail in the alley
someone can die, but the street go on again.

Hitler and others, those pipsqueak voices,
can twitter from speakers. I can look back
from hills beyond town, and every person
and all the alleys, and even the buildings
except the church be hidden in leaves.

This can happen, my parents laughing
because they have already won. And I can
study and grow up and look back and call "Wait!"
and run after their old green car
and be lost again.

Whose Tradition?

It is time—past time—for critics to accept a change that has come about in current poetry. Today a grotesque discrepancy is widening between critical formulations and what thousands of people are experiencing in their reading and writing. The "tradition" from which "individual talents" are deriving has transformed, but the old terminology is lingering and making a separation between writers and the authorities who identify and teach and analyze their work.

Today students all over the country are entering poetry, the reading and writing of it, as an immediate part of their lives. They lavish around in the lines; they swim in the language. They are finding their own central impulses and inventing their own felt sentences in ways other than ways assumed in the past. It is simply not true, for instance, that young students rely on a knowledge of "literature" to enable their entry into poetry—rather, it is the other way round. They rely on talk, their own, and the talk around them. Their writings, and speakings, are like little explosions of discovery, and they delight in those little explosions in talk and in writings of those ignorantly delighting around them.

If young students dive into poetry writing and chanting and reading without using the guidance of the literary tradition, how about older students? Yes—

they too have shaken off the bindings: they read and write a language that grows from daily experience rather than from literary experience. And it is no longer enough to say that the words in use are daily words—the change is greater than that. It is now true that the universe from which we speak is the universe of immediacy, the realm of conversation. Poems are intervals of freedom and excitement in the language that even the youngest and most "uneducated" flourish in.

"Tennis with the net down!" some will charge. It is time to mention that poetry is not tennis, that there are games so important that nothing less than everything in your experience is sufficient to bring along for your involvement. The energy and excitement and flow of realization that language offers is not a derivative from rules and studies. Poetry comes from the continuous adventure of finding for yourself the opportunities that surface when with your own feelings you accept new ideas never before encountered. Poetry is not a going back, but a going forward.

Our whole culture has shifted, and it has shifted not so much in a way that neglects the past as in a way that realizes even in that past a hidden value in poetry: poetry has always been a whole torrent of experience continually outflanking what went before. Even those of us who are critics, teachers, scholars, have always trafficked in something much more precious than our rules could identify; and now with the help of kindergartners, protesters, joshing conversationalists, and disporting scholars, we have glimpsed how language belongs to all of us, and poetry does too. Those who would package it, even if the packaging is validated by scholarship, have been left with the wrappings in their hands and the essence at large in the world around them.

To test some of these claims, visit your local grade

school. Consult your local poet. Thousands enter poetry today by starting from where they are and going in their own direction. People are feeling justified in entering the arts, whatever their talents, and whatever their prospects for being welcomed "at the top." Discovering your own periphery, wherever it is, entices you along; and that enticement is other than a competitive enticement; it is other than the "succeeding" motive; it is a long way other than watching over your shoulder to see how models have acted.

To conceptualize these new ways is hazardous: misunderstandings flourish. For many concerned people the new ways seem to endanger quality, culture, order. Does the prevalence of the new attitude really reduce chances for effective communication? No—the exhilaration of discovery, the variety that comes as a result of being yourself—these benefits are so important and so effective that they bring results that are truly original, more exploratory and satisfactory by far than the "competing-with-models" formula. Using the tradition that comes from all you experience, rather than just from the experience established by study, enables human involvement from the beginning, a validating in terms of your own life. Top accomplishment is not by any means endangered by the recognition that your actions must spring from where you live. You accept leads that take you to unrecognized results. In the arts you must stand fast, accept the chances that the moment brings. To curry favor by saying what you do not mean, or what you do not feel, is as damaging in poetry as it is in politics or business or other parts of life. You can become a lost soul in literature just as surely as you can in any activity where you abandon yourself to the decisions of others. Technique used for itself will rot your soul.

To attack current formulations about poetry suggests the need for alternative formulations, but the new is hard to say without affronting traditionalists. How can we sort out, carefully, what is actually happening? How can we begin to pick up a vocabulary and a set of priorities to suit what is more of a developing feeling than it is a completed change? How can we be kind enough to accept guidance from those who have invested in the past, and still be clear and helpful enough to let them know that something that is indeed new has happened?

As a beginning—poetry today takes in more than the place it has in the view of traditionalists. Poetry today grows from a tradition that is wider than just the sequence of poems we inherit. The language all speakers use is the tradition. The talk around us holds millions of unfound bonuses, many lurking effects that the inventor of the sonnet never got around to recognizing. There are surprises in syllables, rhymes too subliminal for embodiment in rules. There is a tradition yeasting around and changing and enlivening language. Classroom and formal approaches touch only a small part of the great province available. All of us, scholars and all, lean over the desk after class and relax into the originality of conversation. We are briefed by authority but extended by company. The new poetry frisks and risks outside; its authority has to be proved again and again in the never-before-felt moment it happens to find itself in. Those who bring their trained recognitions and forms for reacting to a party have not joined the alive party that human beings create when they accept what emerges from what is always new.

Here are two attempts to depart from current ways, and to confront what poetry feels like among many students and writers.

First, suppose you had a chance to work with someone who would correct your writing into publishability. This person would be efficient, knowing, memorable, valid: an accomplished writer. In the company of this person you could go confidently into the center of current acceptance; you would quickly learn what brings success in the literary scene.

Now suppose another kind of associate. This one would accompany you as you discovered for yourself whatever it is that most satisfyingly links to your own life and writings. You would be living out of your own self into its expression, almost without regard to the slant or expectation or demands of editors and public.

Let there be no mistake about it: a large and significant, and I believe most significant, group of writers today would prefer the second kind of company. There is an abiding interest in the developing forward of the speaker and writer; "correction," "coaching," even "guidance," except of the most sensitive sort—that is not the point. Poetry locates with the individual and in the individual's own choices and responses.

Here is a second way to identify current realizations about poetry and how it grows from a new acceptance of what a poem is. This time we'll turn from the practice of doing poetry to an assessment of the product: a poem is anything said in such a way or put on the page in such a way as to invite from the hearer or reader a certain kind of attention. Not the form, not the topic, but the circumstances or conditions will mark the difference between poetry and prose. We signal that we are doing something special, and we listen or read with a readiness to accept something special. It is hard to spell out more specifics about what a poem is today, without limiting the state of readiness that is needed in accepting it. And the state of readiness is the essential factor.

Finally—put the net down: here comes a story or dream or myth that intends to give a feeling about what poetry does today. This attempt flows on and finds its way as it goes. This may even be a poem:

There is a dream going on while I am awake.
Because I must pay attention to what
is happening around me, I am unconscious
of the dream. When I sleep, the daylight
things fade out and the perpetual dream
surfaces fully and is memorable.
When I die, the dream is the only
thing left. It balloons and fills the world.

As a writer, I coax partly into action
that internally coherent, silent story.
I let my conscious life yield a little,
and a little more, and occasionally a great way,
to my best needs and hopes: whatever
I mean by my best, whatever I mean
by my judgments on the happenings around me,
that center and guide is invited to have its way.

For intervals, then, throughout our lives
we savor a concurrence, the great blending
of our chance selves with what sustains
all chance. We ride the wave and are
the wave. And with renewed belief
inner and outer we find our talk
turned into prayer, our prayer into truth:
for an interval, early, we become at home in the world.

III
Indirections
Interviews, Conversations

Dreams To Have

An Interview with Cynthia Lofsness

Do you read much contemporary poetry?

I do read a lot of contemporary poetry, but it's sort of like nibbling olives or something.

Which contemporary poets do you feel some sort of affinity with?

I like Thomas Hardy and feel much more affinity with him than with any contemporary poet I can think of now . . . of course he was almost contemporary . . . he died in the late 1920s. I understand Thomas Hardy by sympathy. . . . To many he seems kind of pessimistic, but I get a kind of feeling of elation out of Hardy . . . you know, if human beings inhabit that kind of world it's not their fault. And besides, I just follow his sort of totemistic or feeling of natural influences way of living.

You said you liked Hardy "by sympathy." I recall reading somewhere that you said you liked Yeats, but had no sympathy for him.

Yes, that's true. Yeats seems foreign to me. I'm excited by a lot of those violent encounters of images and so on, that he cultivated in his mind, but that kind of recklessness with images for the sake of firework displays in poetry is just foreign to my nature. It's like visiting a quaint and odd person. But when I read Hardy's poems, I keep having that "huh-huh, yes" feeling. The "I understand" feeling.

When did you first realize that you wanted to become a poet?

I've thought about that, and sort of reversed it. My question is "when did other people give up the idea of being a poet?" You know, when we are kids we make up things, we write, and for me the puzzle is not that some people are still writing, the real question is why did the other people stop?

Do you think that getting to know a man through his poems is possible?

It seems to me that poems, and other kinds of art works, are disguises. I don't mean deliberate disguises, but they are created by following out hunches that are not at all ones that are necessarily central feelings, or durable commitments, but just opportunities. At least when I write, I feel like the kind of person who is ready to try all sorts of things.

So you think then that even reading a great deal of a writer may not bring us close to him as a man?

Yes, what we learn is what they've written; but what they are is what they haven't yet written. What they are is sort of why they wrote it. A poem is not a direct revealing of a person. In my way of writing I've compared it to Daniel Boone going over into Kentucky and finding things—Daniel Boone is not Kentucky.

You once said "The influence I feel when I write, the voice I hear most clearly is that of my mother. . . . I don't really hear the voice of T. S. Eliot very much." Could you comment on that further?

Yes. It was part of my general thesis that a writer is really working by means of those things that are closest to him, his sustained immediate feelings. And it's just part of my feeling, and it's also just a statement of what I feel to be the truth, that when I notice little turns of speech, and attitudes toward events and people, I sense the presence of my mother's nature and her way of talking and a certain kind of not very assertive, but nevertheless, tenaciously, noncommittal judgmental element that was in her. Not to assert very much, but on the other hand, to assert what she felt.

What attitude of hers do you think influenced you most?

I think it was an attitude of not being impressed by the sort of stance or posture that most people take. I also remember her listening without making an overt comment, but nevertheless having her judgment about some person or some event. Later she would speak freely about it in a context where it wouldn't hurt the other person.

You mentioned that you didn't hear the voice of T. S. Eliot very much; would you please comment upon two quotes of his from the essay "Tradition and the Individual Talent"?

Yes, I know that essay.

He said, "The progress of an artist is a continual self-sacrifice, a continual extinction of personality. Poetry is not the expression of personality, but an escape from personality." Would you comment upon that?

[Slight laughter] I have kind of a complex reaction to that. I can't feel the separation between the artist and the person in the immediacy of his experience. For me, writing (maybe other art, but I'll stick to writing for this) is a process of relying on immediate pervasive feelings, not an escape from them at all, not at all. . . . However once you enter into what the material is offering to you, you begin to build up something and your creation may seem to others like a disguise or something different, but for me it's like thinking. When I think, I think all sorts of things . . . half of my thoughts are the other extreme from what I finally commit myself to . . . so the poem may be wildly various, but I'm relying on little impulses that seem to me very close, exactly congruent to the self that I use in other negotiations.

How do you feel about the poets writing now?

Of the men writing now, I think the best is . . . the most significant American poet now is Robert Lowell by quite a distance, I think, and I admire or am impressed by, would be more like it, the involvement with his material. It comes right out of a believable complex or tangle of feelings and background, so I would rate him the highest. There are quite a number of current poets I feel congenial about. I like Galway Kinnell. I think I understand him by sympathy. I feel excitement about and a kind of willing participation when I read quite a number of current poets, but I don't think there's a one who is fully sympatico. I don't know how to get at this. . . . They are doing it with their minds or something and Thomas Hardy was doing it with some kind of instinct, and that interests me more.

Would you compare Roethke and Lowell?

There are some things that Roethke did that are very extreme, and in a sense unsurpassed, in the sense that no one else has gone that far beyond certain boundaries. His way of writing, his little sort of lizard flashes into unknown territory are intriguing; but they don't have the kind of cumulative effect or the pervasive involvement with current life that I feel in Lowell's work.

Do you feel that the arts have been dominated by men?

I do feel that the arts have been dominated by men, and I do feel that many injustices have just grown up and been perpetuated through the operation of influences in society that I don't fully understand. But I feel now, and I've felt for a long time, that there are many injustices. I suppose it's obvious that the ratio of the relative number of men and women in the arts, and in other endeavors too, is pretty largely a function of this endemic discrimination that's been going on. But I myself have admiration for many women writers.

Do you think there has ever been a major American woman poet?

Yes, I think Emily Dickinson is a major American poet. Period.

And the best woman poet writing today in your opinion?

Uhmmmmm . . . American?

Or English.

[Laughter] . . . I was looking for some help . . . to figure out . . . you know . . . let my mind range more.

Perhaps if I rephrased that. Do you think any woman writing today shows signs of greatness . . . or the possibility of becoming a major American poet of the stature of say, Emily Dickinson?

I don't think there is any poet writing today, man or woman, who is as great as Emily Dickinson.

Not even Robert Lowell?

[Laughter] Yes, not even Robert Lowell. But, of course, Emily Dickinsons don't happen very often. And as for American women novelists, I have an immediate allegiance for someone like Willa Cather . . . I think she is a great writer . . . her novels are solid, and great. And when I read back in English literature to the nineteenth century, I have great admiration for George Eliot, for instance, I think that she is, that her novels are, first rate, and of course, Jane Austen too. In a way, I seem to be avoiding the current scene, which I don't want to do; it's just that there are a number of women poets, I think, today who are right in there with men poets, it's just that the whole literary scene is too near and blurred for me to separate them out the way I separate out Thomas Hardy and Emily Dickinson . . . to them I give my allegiance.

You mentioned Willa Cather . . . she wrote about the area in which you grew up didn't she?

Yes . . . the plains . . . but she also wrote about Mexico and Canada.

Did you read her when you were quite young?

Yes, I did . . . and my mother read her. Come to think of it, my mother's taste in stories in general and in novels is very much like my own. And she'd read books over and over again, and I sort of understand that.

Do you read books again and again?

Yes, yes.

Which ones?

Well, I probably know a lot of *Huckleberry Finn* by heart, which I like, and I've read Dickens, and I read people like Walter Scott with a great deal of gusto. People today think it doesn't go fast enough, but I think it goes too fast. [Laughter] I like to relish those slow, expansive, luxurious novels.

In a late poem, "Let Them Alone," Robinson Jeffers says speaking of poets "Let him alone. . . . He can shake off his enemies but not his friends." Would you comment on that?

I don't feel the menace . . . I don't feel that my friends are a menace . . . but on the other hand, I'm not a poet like Robinson Jeffers. I think I understand why he says this, and it does seem to me that many writers, artists, and intellectuals, of all kinds, are victims of people around them, but of course it's a mutual thing. I mean they're willing victims, that's why they're victims. I mean victims in the sense that they get to needing immediate reactions from human beings . . . they get to feeling lonely, and they keep wanting to check what they're doing with all their friends, and that doesn't seem to me to be a good thing to do. I would like to be like the person who raises vegetables. I don't have to run out and show someone passing in the street how good my onions are . . . they're just growing, that's all . . . nothing especially remarkable.

What if you take Jeffers's statement in light of say grants and fellowships, and awards; do you think they can have, besides the beneficial aspects, any detrimental results?

I think they could have detrimental results . . . almost any good thing could, but grants could, if a person begins to organize his life so as to sustain his ability to get grants, then that's one kind of distraction from the pure following out of what he's doing. So I think it's a little bit better to have some kind of a job, some kind of check that you count on, some kind of vocation that won't engulf all of your life. But, I keep telling myself that a grant, now and then, is not too corrupting.

The question that I probably can't phrase as well as I'd like to concerns the commitments you mentioned awhile back . . . commitments, as I see them, to the human family, to civilization. Whether one calls it commitments or appropriately the title of your new book Allegiances, *it's probably as strong or stronger in your work as can be found in the work of any poet writing today. At what time were you conscious that that was the fork in the road that you took?*

Well, I'm not sure I've been conscious of that as a commitment. To me it's more like . . . the book doesn't say commitments, it just says *Allegiances*, and this is more like something that comes naturally to a person. It's like feeling at home in the world. . . . I do feel at home in the world. It's like assuming good will on the part of other people—I tend to do that. It's like a kind of level look at every day's experience as it comes at you and welcoming it. I feel that . . . you know . . . not alienation, not resentment, or rebellion, but a kind of acceptance and even a hopeful acceptance that enjoys being part of the human family . . . something like that.

Your poem, "Traveling Through the Dark," seems to speak more of a commitment, however. Especially the line "I think hard for us all."

Yes. You know that is not a poem that is written to support a position that I have chosen, it's just a poem that grows out of the plight I am in as a human being.

But it is definitely to people as versus animals and the world of nature, that your allegiances lie.

I can't help feeling a little bit closer to people than to animals.

Have you ever felt in agreement with Whitman in his "Song of Myself" when he states that he feels as though he could turn and live with the animals, they are so placid and self-contained . . . not a one of them gripes . . . .

They're not whimpering and so on. Yes, of course I've felt that but that's just a part of myself that springs out of some temporary feeling of pique or perception or human encounter. I would have that feeling in an extreme of thinking, but I wouldn't have it as a set policy . . . mostly I'd rather live with people.

What causes or gives rise to this pique . . . what disappoints you most often in other people?

Well, I find myself stumbling into human situations that are like traps already set, you know. Maybe people's resentments are built up by conditions that I haven't anticipated, so I don't always meet that good will and welcome into the family kind of feeling—that is upsetting to me—and if I have a principle about it, it is well to remember that this came about through circumstances that you didn't anticipate. Your job is not necessarily resentment, but understanding and hope for better luck next time . . . something like that.

You once mentioned that you like the work of Robinson Jeffers very much . . . and yet so many of his ideas are almost polar opposites of yours.

When I read Robinson Jeffers I have a steady sense of where he is . . . sort of like where the north star is, or anything that's pretty far off, but definite. And his poems express often what many people feel is a violence, pessimism, and so forth, yet they spring from a point of view which for me is very steady and understandable. After all, those extreme statements come from some kind of commitment and involvement on his part. I mean . . . it's sort of like Jonathan Swift . . . if he didn't care, he wouldn't write that way. . . . He cares. . . . I understand.

What do you see as the main advantages of working as a college teacher?

I like the academic world, myself. I think that many people outside it have forgotten or have never fully realized the great advantages in the academic world. You meet people in your daily life who are committed to a way of proceeding that I find very congenial . . . that is, they are looking for help in revising tentative conclusions . . . they are not doctrines and policies that are deciding once and for all . . . it's kind of an adventurous search among like-minded people and to me this is very important. Out in the world, in the world outside, you keep meeting people who are like robots. They are committed to something they're programmed for, for their life work, but in the academic world, our life work is a steady process of findings, discoveries, readiness. . . . I think it's a great place.

What disadvantages do you see in the academic world?

Well the academic world is always changing—that is, the people you meet are always changing. For me one of the trials is that I'm surrounded by people I don't know well enough to have a close relationship with—I'm thinking about the student generations who pass by so fast. On the other hand, there are a lot of them, so in a way, your contacts with people are all diluted and changed all the time . . . and my instinct or my nature is for steadier, fewer people. I'd rather either not know someone at all or know them very well. ... You know that's easy, but in the academic life it's always that sort of in between.

What do you learn from your students?

For me the students are not a special group ... I mean they are an intelligent pretty lucky kind of people usually. College students are a pretty lucky group, in general, and so it's fun to know them, but I don't quite share the opinion that some people have that every student generation seems to be a whole lot better than the one before in all sorts of ways. I have reservations about that. I think what we learn from each other is that we are all somewhat fallible. I learn particular things from students—you can always learn particulars from different people, so I don't class them as a group—they're just too transient to be of the greatest value, but they are a great potential.

What are your goals as a teacher?

Well, I just sort of stumbled into teaching ... and my goals in teaching are more of an incidental thing. ... I have an interest in literature and writing, so I'm hired to be on a campus where some others may have that convergent interest, and our interest is not so much in each other, as it is in literature and writing ... it seems to me, or at least this is the stance I take.

You mentioned that you just sort of stumbled into teaching; what had you done prior to teaching?

I tried many things ... I worked as a laborer, I worked for the forest service, which I liked ... I worked one year as a kind of secretary and man of all work in the office of a church relief organization, Church World Service, and I liked that year. . . . There are a lot of things I haven't done, but that I'm thinking of doing. . . . I like the idea of photography, or farming. . . . I would like to have some kind of skill that would make it easy for me to know when I have finished a job . . . one of the maddening things about the academic life is that you never know when you've done the job . . . there is no feeling of closure, and I like to be able to let it go click.

In the anthology, Naked Poetry, *you included a small article that contained the statement, "the feel of composition is more important than any rule or prescribed form."*

Yes, yes.

This seems to say to me then, that emphasis placed on technique is wrong, so I wonder then what is your opinion of writers' workshops, or the poetry workshops and other type apprentice-type programs?

Well, I have to say something that will probably seem contradictory and I don't know what to do about it, except just be honest. That is, I've liked writers' workshops, I've served easy time . . . many schools and many jobs like them. If something is pleasant and seems to be productive, I can't help feeling that it's all right, that it's doing some good. On the other hand, I continue to be puzzled by what people mean by technique. . . . I just can't come at it that way. I just don't know what they mean . . . each poem seems to me to be a new kind of plunge.

I would define technique as a belief on the part of the poet that there are certain rules or forms into which his ideas must be channeled for proper expression. A belief

*that there is a proper "framework," into which he must
fit his specific feelings . . .*

Then I see why I don't understand technique. When I'm
writing, I'm not at all trying to fit in any forms, though
I think it's easy to do, by the way. That doesn't seem to
me the crucial or essential thing, and I suppose this feel-
ing is the source of that quote about the feel of compo-
sition. It's not a technique, it's a kind of stance to
take toward experience, or an attitude to take toward
immediate feelings and thoughts while you're writing.
That seems important to me, but technique is something
I believe I would like to avoid.

*What then is your opinion of the Black Mountain school
of poetry with their breathed lines . . . so many breaths
per line, etc.?*

I read, reviewed in fact, Charles Olson's *Selected Writ-
ings*, with an introduction by Creeley, a few years ago,
and when I had the assignment to review this book, I
thought, now's my chance to learn what this is all
about. You know, I had been hearing about it all my
life and sort of giving a general assent, not being nega-
tive, so I read it carefully, and I thought that many of
the positions taken about writing, about poetry, lines,
and so on, seemed quite congenial to me . . . it didn't
seem like news . . . it seemed like, yeah, that's what I
thought everyone thought.

*Do you think it has produced good poets . . . would you
consider Creeley and Olson and Wieners to be good
poets?*

I think Creeley is a good poet. I can't feel at all per-
suaded by Olson as a poet. . . . I just don't feel engaged

at all . . . it's like a passing of each other in the corridors on different levels, or something, and so for the others. But Creeley I do understand. I can't help feeling that there are more differences among those people than their syndicating themselves together would lead one to believe. It seems to me that they are separate writers who happen to have a label.

What do you think of Robert Frost? Why do you think he was singled out as THE American poet?

Well, I can't help thinking that part of Frost's centrality in American life comes from qualities that are not necessarily good, or not necessarily important for poetry. He lived a long time, he showed up well in photographs, and you know, he came from the right part of the country. . . . His reputation just followed the tide of the pioneers and so on. [Pause]

What about his reputation as the wise old New Englander, and the Backwoods Prophet?

[In a sharp tone] I don't feel he was wise at all, his political advice seemed to me poisonous, and his influence on politics, if he had any, just seems to me feedback of stereotypes. So I don't consider him a seer at all or wise man or prophet or anything like that. But he was a tenacious old guy who wrote some interesting poems.

I would be interested in knowing if you feel you have any flaws as a writer, either conspicuous ones or secret ones?

Yes I think I have many flaws as a writer. . . . I usually try not to brood about these things, because it doesn't do much good. On the other hand, it might be good to think about it now and then. One of them is just limitations—just not being fast enough . . . or ranging enough in thought, just not being rich enough intellectually. . . .

You write a lot. . . .

Well, yes, I see what you mean . . . yeah, yeah . . . of course, anyone though, can write a lot . . . but is what you write a product of real flashes of realization? of imagination and so on? I feel that certainly I am heavily burdened with limits. What I think of . . . I don't think of enough! and I don't perceive relations between things vividly enough, coherently enough, cumulatively enough. So most of the flaws I think of if I stop and ask myself—I don't feel any stabs of lost opportunity; it's not that at all.

Do you have any regrets about your writing or your career?

Well I don't have regrets in the sense of thinking . . . if only I had done so and so, I'd be a major poet, or something like that. No, I don't think I could have managed it any better . . . you see what I mean. Alas . . . I can't blame any particular mistakes, it's just kind of a steady limitedness. That's what I feel.

If you were to be remembered by only one poem or say, if only one poem of yours could survive for future generations, which one would you select?

I'm not sure I can figure this out, but I do have an immediate impulse of the kind of poem that would immediately occur to me would be some little sort of nagging thing that no one would think very much of at any certain time, but they would never quite get rid of—it would just be there. And I think of a poem of mine that's not necessarily at all the poem, but at the end it's a poem about dandelions on the church lawn. . . . I forget how it goes, but at any rate the very last line . . . these dandelions go floating away, and they are saying their little song: "God is not big, He is right." [Laughter]

Do you find any pattern of ideas recurring in your work?

Well one of the elements is not a pattern of ideas, but a feeling of coziness or a feeling of being at home. It's like the delight of having shelter in a storm or it's like the feeling of becoming oriented where you've been temporarily disoriented . . . or something like that. I would expect to find that showing up in the patterns because that is what I like to think I like to find.

Your father is so frequently present in many of your poems . . . I wondered if you would tell me a little about him . . . how he influenced you and your feelings toward him?

Well, I feel very positive in favor of my father. I've talked to quite a number of writers who have felt rebellion. My father was always very sympathetic and helpful and sort of a level equitable person throughout my life, steady with counsel, but not intruding. All my life long I've had a feeling of . . . not of rebellion, because there was no oppression . . . there was a kind of interest and even surprise and delight, but no oppression at all. I feel very positively about him and I suppose it shows up in the poetry.

What do you think your father would have thought of Allegiances?

You mean the new book?

Yes.

I think he would have liked it. And I think he would have liked it for a reason that is inherent in the book and in my own feeling about it, I believe, and that is he would never have assumed that any one separate poem is the total statement of a person, you know, they are try-outs. He tried things. He would write things, read things, talk easily . . . even recklessly, and assume good will on the part of the hearer and the other speakers. And I believe the book is like that.

Did he also write poetry?

He's been known . . . he did a little bit of that and he tried various things . . . and he always had an interest in what other people tried in that regard.

Have you done any translating?

Yes . . . I tried some Spanish, which I know, a little bit, I took it in school . . . and I've tried translating some French, which I had to learn to read, sort of, and I've recently been engaged in translating from the Urdu. Do you know about the Urdu?

Ghalib?

Yes, the Ghazals of Ghalib, and this was just because —I mean all those translations came about just because people suggested to me that I try it, and somebody else helps, and gives the first version, and I try to make an English poem out of it.

You have translated from the Spanish poets ... would you include any of the great Spanish poets among those you greatly admire ... men such as Neruda, Lorca, Vallejo, etc.?

Even though I tried to translate those people, and had some of the translations published, I can't feel that I know their poems well enough to have very much judgment about how I feel about them. All I know is that some of the prose bringings-over into English were interesting enough to be occasions for interesting projects for me to write. But I don't know them well enough to judge them, so I couldn't include them.

Would you please compare the creative powers involved in writing your own poems and those involved in translating?

I always feel reluctant about going into translations ... it's like doing a job whereas writing poems is more like fishing, you know, a sport. Strangely, I feel more secure about doing translations, because I know I'm going to come out with something; but I don't feel a sense of adventure and that's a distraction.

Would you tell me something about your work habits?

Yes, I get up early in the morning, before anyone else, so that there is a space of time that won't be interrupted ... it's quiet, I'm wide awake, and then I just start to write whatever occurs to me, no matter how trivial, in order to get into motion, and the process of writing calls up other things, and a kind of train sets in, the sequence that comes about because I'm in motion. And every morning there is something to write about because it doesn't have to be much. It can be anything, there's always something.

Every morning? Are there mornings when you can't write?

There are never mornings when I can't write. I think there are never mornings that anybody "can't write." I think that anybody could write if he would have standards as low as mine. [Strange laughter]

What about revisions, and reworking your poems . . . do you tend to work on several poems at once, do you wait until one is finished, do you start at the beginning and keep rewriting, etc.?

I don't have any feeling about refraining from working on several at once . . . I mean if I'm enticed by something, I may write something different tomorrow from what I'm writing today, and so, there may be two or three things going and maybe none of them ever gets finished, but maybe all of them might. . . . So I think maybe three or four . . . it just depends upon how much distraction one individual can stand. So I have all sorts of things just moving along, maybe, and I do revise in the sense I do go back over what I write, but it doesn't seem like a different process. It's just the same process, going back through the same terrain again . . . seeing if the signals are different, and then seeing if the signals are different the next time. And every now and then, you may get a little nudge of a new idea, or adjustment, and you do it, and that makes it easier the next time. And finally when you run out of profitable moves, or when you are enticed away from it, then it's done. If it's done.

In your lecture, you referred to abandoning poems.

Yes . . . I was remembering an Auden quote I heard that "poems are not finished, they're just abandoned." And I do understand this, because I don't know when a work is finished . . . it's always subject to revision.

Have you ever gone back and worked on a poem that you once considered finished?

No, because after they are so old—maybe six or seven days old—they for some reason . . . always just seem to have been written by somebody else. I'm more interested in something newer than that. So I've never gone back to do extensive revisions of old work.

Today when there seems to be almost more literary criticism published than literature, I would be interested in your opinion of the critics who feel they can approach the "man behind the work" through his work. Do you think this is a valid assumption?

I don't think they can ever get there. For me, the difficulty of the critic, the incapacity to ever get there, is no reflection at all upon the individual critic or anything like that. It's just that the process of writing is a kind of weaving forward from one thing to another, and to go back through that process of writing and try to unravel it, being another person with another sensibility, and different sets of experiences. . . . You can see the hazards that multiply.

You mentioned in an interview back in 1962 that you felt alien as a poet from the rest of the community. Do you feel this way now?

No, not so much. I did feel removed, because to me, at that time, it seemed odd to take time to write and since then, I found that the community forgives more than I thought. . . . That is, I have learned that there are lots of other people doing things that are not so ordinary, and I think that was part of my provinciality about the complexities of society.

Why did you wait so long to publish your first book?

Yes! People said, you know, you waited until you were into your thirties, or something like that, but I wasn't waiting! I just didn't have a publisher! I kept sending out poems, and . . . I don't know how to feel when someone talks to me about waiting, because it certainly wasn't any policy on my part, but on the other hand, I don't feel that anyone was slighting me. It's just that I had the poems there, and maybe I didn't always send them to the right place; it just didn't happen, that's all.

In 1962, you characterized yourself as "one of the quiet of the land, even somewhat conservative." Would you describe yourself that way today?

Well, I think that holds up better than some of the things that I said in that interview. Yes, at least as conservative as possible . . . you know, I don't like the idea of going around looking for opportunities to disagree, and so I feel like a person who would like to conform so far as possible. You know of course there are limits, and so I would like to reduce the attempt to be rebellious without reducing the willingness to take meaningful stands on essential things. Something like that.

You did take a meaningful stand by refusing to serve in World War II.

Yes, yes, there are some things that one should just never do.

What led you to make the decision to be a conscientious objector?

Well in World War II that position was an odder one than it is now. And I suppose family background had some part in it and a kind of feeling of assuming good will on the part of other people, and being puzzled about how a line on a map kept people over there from being also people of good will. And my parents were always skeptical about general judgments around them ... they were reserved about accepting patterns of thought without a little juggling of their own. They were always reading foreign books. And I just could not come down to nationalistic location for virtue. So I was a conscientious objector.

You also said that you believed "that people, in their best selves are social and mutually helpful, and that any other policy would be a kind of suicide." You continued that thought by saying that "a long term cold war, or a cold anything, is to foster among us a paralysis of those qualities on which we commonly and ultimately have to rely." That was 1962. Instead of a cold war, we now [1972] have a genocidal war raging in Asia ... what's to become of us ... any predictions, etc.?

Yes. [Sighing] Well, my impulse is to feel uncomfortable about that formulation, you know, it sounds more sure of things than I really am . . . although events seem to bear it out all too well. . . . I mean a long enduring kind of conflict has brought us to feeling suspicion among ourselves, and divisiveness, and it's very hard to maintain the sense of community that seems to me to be necessary for the health of the country or in a society when we are torn. And some of us sadly forced to be in munitions and actually in fighting and so on. So I don't feel that much of a prophet. . . . I suspect that was pretty much formulated by the person who did the interview because it's his position, but I can't disagree . . . it sounds a little more assured than I feel myself.

In reviewing The Rescued Year, *Louis Simpson stated that you were a "True Poet," and said that "if ever this country is going to have a sense of itself, it will be through work like Stafford's." What "sense of itself" would you like to give to the American people? What quality or qualities would you like them to recognize and/or come to terms with in themselves?*

Well a judgment like this about poetry puts me in a strange spot because when I write I don't have any program, any idea of any purpose to tell the American people about themselves, or anything like that, or how they ought to be. But instead it's just like groping forward into an experience of my own . . . that is, here a critic has judged the product, and I feel flattered that he would notice the product and judge it so favorably. But I really didn't write it with the intention that is ascribed to me . . . so I don't know what to do. I think critics have often manifested the essentially random nature of critical remarks. It's hard to get parallel to the writer's way of working, so you keep crossing his poems and you say things that are true, but

I think the writer keeps thinking, or at least I keep thinking, all right, all right, but then I think other things too. In general, I think poetry criticism, as written by poets, they do know the most about it, but they're also, most of them, too careful, too benevolent. I don't mean that they ought to be mean to each other, but we have to learn to accept the person's acceptance and rejection. A critic ought to be at least as mean as a poet. And most poets, when they turn critic, either turn entirely mean, except to their gang, or they get too soft.

Quite honestly, I'm not trying to pester you, but if we could go back to Simpson's remark about this country hopefully having a sense of itself. Your poetry aside, what would you, William Stafford, like the American people to recognize about themselves?

I would like to see them recognize the complexities faced by other people. I would like them to have an increased sense of how issues bring about alienation between groups that are self-justifying . . . somehow, or to put it another way, I would like to try to help the American people to see the possibilities of reconciliation. I don't find myself in harmony with the current style of the politics of overcoming . . . I have a kind of feeling for empathy with others, including extremely different others.

Do you believe the spirit of assuming good will on the part of others, and the other goals you just mentioned can be achieved in the present structure or framework we live in, in this country?

Not entirely, apparently, but somewhat, yes. For, the world is a somewhat place, and ah . . . little bonuses and benefits are very much to be desired. And in order to achieve the unattainable, we may destroy little pieces of the good life, and I believe we can increase the good life by treasuring the little pieces of it. This is a kind of Burkean position.

The little things that make up the good life ... what are the little pieces of the good life for you? What brings you happiness?

I would like to be able to meet all kinds of people, including the enemy ... under conditions, I would like to maximize the conditions of meeting them so as to bring us to perceive our mutual interests, rather than to drive them farther away. It's a way of life that hasn't prevailed, it hasn't brought peace into the world, but we share that frustration with a lot of other people.

Do you think that one man really has another man as his enemy? Do you think we can call other people enemies?

I'm reluctant to do that ... instead, I would like to make that kind of reach I was talking about, that empathy, to understand.

Stanley Moss, in reviewing The Rescued Year *in the* New Republic, *said that "Stafford is engaged in a battle for his soul ... he is closer to Faust than to Job."*

[Chortling laughter, as if hearing it for the first time] Well, I do like that idea ... and actually, in my own life, and in my writing, I do feel exhilaration of a kind of promise and partial fulfillment, at times a kind of a struggle . . . but I'm kind of surprised that someone would see it in the poems. Again, I read a critic, and I sort of like what he says, but I don't know whether it applies more to me than to somebody else. I suspect that it is something that the critic is doing. Usually what the critic identifies is something that he either wants to do, or doesn't want to do. I mean, he has some kind of orientation toward the topic himself, and he finds it in the poet, and since we all have many things in us, I'm not surprised to find myself agreeing, but not entirely agreeing.

So you feel closer to Faust than to Job . . . what if I were to ask you to identify with one person from the Bible; whom would you pick?

Ohhh . . . I don't know if they have any of my class in the Bible . . . I really hadn't thought about this . . . if I had my druthers, I would like to be somewhat like Moses . . . but, that's not really my role. Ah . . . I really don't know.

Well, in reading the Bible, are there any persons with whom you feel like exclaiming "Yes, me too!"

Different moods, different persons. I suppose sometimes I feel like those people driven out into the wilderness, you know. I never do feel a mystic, or like one who perceives the truth. I would feel more like some kind of wanderer, blunderer, but nevertheless, a benevolent wanderer or blunderer.

In writing about your poem, "Fifteen," Stanley Moss made a rather unusual remark. He said that he "sud-

denly realized that someone like the bleeding motor-
cyclist crashes into almost all of Stafford's poems, and
that motorcyclist is the poet himself."

[Laughter] Oh ho ... I see ... Yes ... suddenly I do
remember other poems where people do come crashing
in.

He says that you are "deceptively simple."

[Laughter] ... Oh, I like that ... I think it's true. I
think he's right. I am deceptively simple ... in other
words, I'm not really simple. Okay, all right.

You said the other day that if writing is continual, there
is more of a chance of something happening ...

Yes ... I've experienced that the activity of writing
does make things happen. ... That's the way ideas come
about for me ... through a willing acceptance of sub-
ideas that aren't really dignified enough for most people
to pay any attention to, but if I begin to pay attention
things always come. ... It's not writing from a reservoir;
it's like engaging in an activity out of which things
come.

What question didn't I ask that you would like to
include?

Well for one thing, I would like to disassociate myself
from taking any kind of stance that would imply that
being a writer is assuming a power of guidance or
insight or anything like that. I'm not that kind of
writer. It seems to me a writer is engaged in adventuring
into the language and all sorts of things occur to him

or should occur to him, that's his job; the judging of these things, the selection of these things, and conduct in light of these things, is everybody's job. And I don't believe in discipleship or even leadership, or anythng like that. Maybe this is one of the things I get from my parents . . . a kind of readiness, even when I was very small, for them to accept some things I could see that they couldn't see, and for me to accept some things they could see that I couldn't see. There was an easy give and take. I remember when I was a little kid, my father took me out for a hike in the country and we were looking for a hawk that we thought had landed in a line of cottonwood trees . . . and he said, "Now Billy, look carefully, in these trees—you may be able to see the hawk better than I can." For me, this is just a little emblem in my life . . . because I remember the jolt I felt: could I see the hawk before my father would? And his tone of voice just said, "Maybe you can, maybe you can't . . . give it a try."

Finding What the World Is Trying To Be
An Interview with Sanford Pinsker

I was very struck by the final line of "Vocation," the concluding poem in your prizewinning volume Traveling Through the Dark: *"Your job is to find what the world is trying to be." Your father's advice in the poem seems as good a way as any of describing what you seem to be doing in the book.*

Well, the word "vocation" means a calling. It sees writing as an exploration, a discovery of process. I don't see writing as a communication of something already discovered, as "truths" already known. Rather, I see writing as a job of experiment. It's like any discovery job; you don't know what's going to happen until you try it. All life is like that. You don't make life be what you've decided it *ought* to be. You find out what life is *trying* to be. And I'm glad that you feel the book's last line is picking up some extra benefits. I certainly had the feeling of going out at the end of *Traveling Through the Dark*, of leaving things on an open-ended note.

Beyond a sense of a life devoted to remaining open to experience, did you have any other principles of arrangement where that book was concerned?

Well, I think there are some general principles that might apply. For example, I try to keep poems that are near each other from detracting. Partly it's a negative consideration: Be sure not to have a sequence in which one poem might sabotage another or create some unintentionally ludicrous effect. I'm always scared about that. I don't know if it's very important, but it is one of the superstitions I have. Certainly the first poem of the book—"Traveling Through the Dark"—and the last one—"Vocation"—were carefully chosen. A person might pick up your book and look at the beginning to see if he likes it. And then he might look at the end to see if he *still* likes it—so if you have a couple of good poems, one at the beginning and one at the end, that might be a good thing.

Were there any notions on your part of, say, a sequential development of the poems between, some spine that would connect the individual poems throughout into a unified whole?

At the time of writing there certainly wasn't. But when I was collecting the poems together—and this is true for every book I've done—I did have some sense of a pattern or a *program* in the book. It doesn't have to be very strong, though, and maybe it's just in my own mind.

I take it, then, that you would agree with a statement Saul Bellow once made. He said that he never knows what he's going to do until he's done it.

I'm glad to hear that about him. I didn't know that, but I would agree. It's partly just *true*, but it's also part of my own program. I don't *want* to know because I think of writing as a *creative* act. That is, things happen that just wouldn't have happened if you hadn't started to write. I have that feeling about any individual poem. It comes about with my engagement in the making of the poem.

Auden and Roethke have both said that when they finish a poem that they know is really *good, the satisfaction quickly fades into an anxious question: "Maybe this is the last time?"*

Those poor guys. I can't imagine what kind of anxiety-ridden life that would be. My own feeling is that we don't have to worry about that. Will we think of something else? *Sure* we will. We always do. I do not at all have that feeling. I meet people who have done something good and they want to cherish it, to hoard it somehow—because it might be the only time in their lives. . . . Well, I have this feeling: "No, no, no" . . . all these things are expendable and the more expendable you keep feeling these things are, the more likely you are to have things happen to you.

It doesn't sound as if you are troubled by writing blocks.

Writing blocks? I don't believe in them.

But what if somebody has one*? Doesn't that person have* to believe in them*? You* may not suffer from them, *but surely other people do.*

No, I've never experienced anything like that. I believe that the so-called "writing block" is a product of some kind of disproportion between your standards and your performance. I can imagine a person beginning to feel that he's not able to write up to that standard he imagines the world has set for him. But to me that's surrealistic. The only standard I can rationally have is the standard I'm meeting right now. Of course I can write. *Anybody* can write. People might think that their product is not worthy of the person they assume they are. But it is.

Aren't you really talking, in a nice way, about vanity?

Yes. I think vanity gets in your way. You begin to feel you've accomplished something once—and you get afraid that you won't be able to accomplish it again, at least right now. So you don't go into anything. But my own feeling is that you should be more willing to forgive yourself. It really doesn't make any difference if you are good or bad today. The *assessment* of the product is something that happens *after* you've done it. You should simply go ahead and *do* it. And do it, I might add, without being critical.

Is there any point, though, in the history of a given poem—draft after draft—when the critical faculties of the poet ought *to intrude?*

If I *had* to choose an answer and there was only one, I'd say "No! There's no point." And that is because I would rather be wholehearted and be welcome about anything I write. The correct attitude to take about anything you write is "Welcome! Welcome!" Once you get yourself into the position of feeling that something that occurs to you is unworthy, well that's tough—because that happens to be what *has* occurred to you.

But don't you revise your own poems?

Well, what I do is revise them *outward.* Usually when somebody says "revise" they think that means "cutting down" or something like that. I feel revise means "More . . . more . . . more." And, of course, there comes a time when you don't force everything into print. That's certainly true in my own case. But the *feeling* at the time is *not* that this poem is bad, but that there must be *other.* And there must be *more.* So I drift back through the poem with something of the same welcoming feeling I had when I began. I may get different signals and change something, but it's not changing things with a stern face. Rather, it's a welcoming one.

Perhaps this sense of "welcome" you speak about is related to my students' sense of you as a very serene, almost unflappable person. I realize this must sound like an awfully dumb question, but how does one go about achieving that sense of inner peace you radiate so naturally?

Well, I have a formula for this that may be just a gimmicky way of explaining it. Anyway, it goes like this: one should lower his standards until there is no felt threshold to go over in writing. It's *easy* to write. You just shouldn't have standards that inhibit you from writing. After all, writing is a creative thing and you ought to get into action.

What about reading other poets, particularly the "great" ones? Couldn't that become an inhibiting factor?

No. I think such reading is harmless. Particularly the reading of excellent models. I think God has put a safety factor in here. You are unable to read up to a standard greater than the standard of yourself. You may feel a good deal of gusto about a great poem, but that's because you are *worthy* of it. You just cannot feel that gusto if you're not worthy. So, if you really do feel that a certain poem is *that* good, you are just about there yourself. I mean, you're that kind of person.

Are you suggesting, then, something like the notion that a good reading of a poem is, in fact, a recreation of it? You know, the sort of thing that allows us to link creative writing with creative reading.

Yes, you don't realize how good something is until you are worthy of it. So I imagine a reader not responding to something that the "big world" would say is great. Now that's not a reflection on the poem. Rather, it's a reflection on him. And, of course, there's a corollary to that: if a person reads a poem and feels its greatness, that's not a reflection on him, it's a *confirmation* of his ability.

In your poem "With Kit, Age 7, At the Beach," the initial lines describe a climb to "the highest dune,/ from there to gaze and come down:" It is a finely rendered, concrete situation, for all its overtones of something "larger" than an excursion to the shore. But I was really struck by the last lines of the poem:

> "How far could you swim, Daddy,
> in such a storm?"
> "As far as was needed," I said,
> and as I talked, I swam.

They turn the poem into something extraordinary.

Yes, I think there is a drastic change there. All the first part of the poem is telling artlessly, directly, simply a succession of encounters in the real world. There's no problem in terms of a reader accepting anything in the early part of that poem: it says we climbed a dune, looked out at the ocean . . . all entirely believable. But the last line—"and as I talked, I swam."—puts the reader in the presence of a statement that *cannot* be taken on the simple level. So he has to make a reversal and accept it as something metaphorical. There's no particular problem about doing this; you simply *have* to. On the literal level it simply won't work. So I *do* feel there is a drastic change. But the whole thing, even from the first. . . . You suggested something about using the landscape there as a model for a deeper meaning. *All* particulars reflect something, if looked at alertly enough. The job in writing is the repeated encounter with particulars. It may be that you hit on a succession of particulars that reinforce each other—and in that case you have a poem.

Does that explain your apparent unhappiness with "Allegiances"?

Yes, it's too doctrinaire. The things I say in the poem— that "It is time for all the heroes to go home," etc.— I do believe them, but on the other hand, not much happens. It's the saying of a whole succession of general truths and I hope that an aesthetic effect comes out of it. But I'm not at all sure and I feel that it's a pretty "relaxed" poem. I feel disquieted about it now.

But aren't there a good many "flat" or bald statements of belief made in contemporary poetry? Some of them are very memorable indeed. I think, for example, of Auden's line: "We must love one another or die."

He didn't like that at the last, though, did he? . . . *I* like it. Well, flat statements are made by people in conditions that induce you to forgive their making the statement. Auden—and all of us—are in a situation where that particular flat statement happens to have a great deal of force. We can say it without thinking that it's a newly discovered truth and still think it's worth saying.

If we can move for just a moment to a poem of yours I like very much—"Traveling Through the Dark." It seems to me that there you stay with the literal situation of the dead deer and the highway without the sort of drastic switch you pull off in the final line of "With Kit, Age 7, At the Beach."

Well, "Traveling Through the Dark" says something drastic at the end too, although it is said in a different way. I mean the whole poem has been leading up to it and it is something that you have to say. But there is a kind of suspense building up as well, because not until you say that last thing—"I thought hard for us all—my only swerving—/then pushed her over the edge into the river."—are all the people involved reconciled that that is going to happen. The whole poem holds back from saying it and then you *do* say it . . . I mean, you *do* it. Maybe this is to the point here: I think poems get themselves written and resolved in various ways. I mean, even if you are a consistent kind of person, lots of things will occur to you. Every poem is different. And you're quite right about the differences in those two poems.

Would it be fair to say that the sort of ambivalent situation you describe in "Traveling Through the Dark" is only resolved, if at all, in the making of a poem about it?

For me, that kind of situation permeates life. Choices are always Hobson's choices. All you have to do is get a little more alert to see that even your best moves are compromises—and complicated. You get some consequences you were aiming for—and some that you weren't.

Isn't poetry—rather than the one-dimensionality of prose—the best way of expressing exactly that?

Maybe that's one of the things that keeps me interested in doing poems. Sometimes the question comes up: "Do you write other things?" And the answer, in my case, is "Yes." And when people ask what especially interests me about poetry, I have various answers. But I believe what you just said—about the multifaceted possibilities of life that a poem might capture if it is successful—is a part of my abiding interest.

Could you even imagine writing "Traveling Through the Dark" as an essay? That is, some prose account of your experience with the deer and the narrow country road?

No. That had to be spare. And to have flying speed as an experience. If you begin to elaborate it, you *may* gain something, but you'll lose the heart of it. That is, what the poem hopefully has.

Yes. That particular poem has the silence so necessary as well as the words. By that I mean, the pauses in "Traveling Through the Dark" may be almost as important as the words chosen.

I like that idea. In fact, you make me think of another thing. It makes me nervous to have people say that poems are made of words. Of course, on one level I know I've got to agree. But poems are also made of *contexts*. If you get certain contexts going, you can make mistakes in wording, in diction. That is, *if* you've got flying speed, some kind of momentum. At least the *feeling* I have is not the feeling of great care that everything is going to explode if I don't have the exact word. In fact, I have the very opposite feeling: even if I have the *wrong* word, this is going to work. I mean, that's the feeling I have when I do a poem. For me, poetry is *not* like the jeweller's craft . . . polishing, polishing, always rubbing it more and more. It's more like the exhilaration of getting somewhere. It's like running fast and your elbows and knees may not always be exactly right . . . but you're really getting somewhere. That's the sort of feeling writing a poem has.

Doesn't that take us right back to the notion on which we began—the business of discovering what the world is trying to be? I suspect if one were to draw a diagram of your work, rather than have it zero in like a jeweller, it would be more like concentric circles moving outward.

Yes. Revising outward. There's always more . . . more.

This may seem like an impertinent question, but in an age when contemporary poets often seem to be super-neurotics in a neurotic world, your apparent lack of anxiety is very striking indeed. How do you manage such calm?

I don't know that there's any distinction about this. At least I *hope* that there isn't any distinction about my attitude toward neurosis. And that is: it's just too bad. You shouldn't have neuroses. You ought to be on the level. You ought to assess the outer world as it is. It's various and exciting enough for a level look to be as exciting as anyone would want in his life. Deranging the senses so as to enhance art has never appealed to me at all. Deranged senses don't bring in enough; arranged senses bring in plenty.

But there are, for example, some very lonely moments in your poetry. I'm thinking now of that serious poem with the wryly funny title "The Only Card I Got on My Birthday Was from an Insurance Man."

Yes. Loneliness is something you'll have plenty of without trying to induce it. You can count on it. As a matter of fact, you don't have to be a neurotic to discover that the world can be a frightening place.

Let me end on a note that might be of special interest to poets less established than yourself. Robert Lowell once said that when he was young, he worried because he couldn't get any *of his poems published. And now he worries even more because he can get* all *of them published. Do you share something of that feeling?*

Well, most of the poems I write I don't send out at all. And of those I send out, maybe a tenth of them finally get published. So that means an awful lot of them get rejected, even ones I think are all right. I look at it this way: you can run across a log pond—you know, where they're floating the logs at a sawmill—by stepping on one log at a time. And if you don't stay on a given log very long, you can go hopping clear across the pond on these logs. But if you stop on one, it'll sink. Sometimes I feel a writer should be like this—that you need your bad poems. You shouldn't inhibit yourself. You need to have your dreams; you need to have your poems. If you begin to keep from dreaming or from trying to write your poems, you could be in trouble. You have to learn how to say "Welcome . . . welcome." Welcome, dreams. Welcome, poems. And then if somebody says "I don't like that dream," you can say "Well, it's my life. I had to dream it." And if somebody else says "I don't like that poem," you can say, "Well, it's my life. That poem was in the way, so I wrote it."

A Prefatory Poem

An Introduction to Some Poems

Look: no one ever promised for sure
that we would sing. We have decided
to moan. In a strange dance that
we don't understand till we do it, we
have to carry on.

Just as in sleep you have to dream
the exact dream to round out your life,
so we have to live that dream into stories
and hold them close at you, close at the
edge we share, to be right.

We find it an awful thing to meet people,
serious or not, who have turned into vacant
effective people, so far lost that they
won't believe their own feelings
enough to follow them out.

The authentic is a line from one thing
along to the next; it interests us.
Strangely, it relates to what works,
but is not quite the same. It never
swerves for revenge,

Or profit, or fame; it holds
together something more than the world,
this line. And we are your wavery
efforts at following it. Are you coming?
Good: now it is time.*

---

*From William Stafford, *Someday, Maybe* (New York: Harper
and Row, 1973).

I Would Also Like To
Mention Aluminum

An Interview with William Heyen and Al Poulin

Poulin: Mr. Stafford, I'd like to begin by asking you about the difference in your own work between the end of conversation and the beginning of poetry.

Yes. Well, for me poetry seems like conversation that has a lot of luck in it. So I feel there's a difference, but not a big distinction. Just some more luck than in conversation. I wouldn't make a great distinction.

Heyen: You said once that "poetry is talking along in our not quite prose way."

I'm afraid sometimes "not-quite-prose" might seem like too great a claim for me to make, because it is sometimes absolutely prose. But as a matter of fact I admire prose and I think I prefer prose to poetry, and I'm forced into poetry by various considerations that don't really have a lot to do with my feeling of the quality or the value of the two kinds of discourse.

P: Someone once said that if you go to a William Stafford reading you're never quite sure when he's reading a poem or when he's talking, that kind of distinction.

You can imagine that I'd have quite a riffle of feelings about this. I don't know which side of various considerations to come down on, because that could sound like a bad thing, but I take it to be a good thing. And if it'd be possible to have a poetry reading, say, in which the remarks that would occur to you would be better than the poems, that would be *great*! That's exactly the kind of reading I'd like to have.

H: Well, I think those "sashays" that you make into prose, *in quotation marks, as you did last night, are very nice too. I mean one of the reasons that the moments of prose and poetry are blurred sometimes is that you say such good things in between.*

I'm not sure about this. You know, I'm an optimist so I try to take things in a happy sense, but sometimes it seems to me that these public occasions are such, and the nature of current poetry is such, that it's possible to convince people in front of you that you are doing something that has significance just by your expression and the deliberation with which you talk. And we are all used to forgiving each other for long passages in our poems anyway, and you sort of lose track about whether you're supposed to be liking the reading as poetry or just accepting it as something that somebody's saying.

H: You know, one of the things it occurred to me to say when you read a poem was "Hey, that doesn't sound like Dylan Thomas or Hopkins at all."

Yes, and I suppose back of this—I'm looking for things back of remarks that are said—back of this is the feeling that—well, there is a topic here for many current writers.

I think—whether we pursue a tradition, and imitate those who have gone before us in writing, or whether, when we write, or when we enter the arts, we are entering with the rest of our lives, and it doesn't make any difference at the moment who has gone before or what the tradition is. I feel like not being dominated by tradition. I realize that we are all *influenced* by tradition, but the feeling at the time is like the feeling of talking, coming out of that tradition into whatever is new.

P: I think one thing that relates to this is your comment that "no one ever promised for sure/that we would sing. We have decided/to moan."

Yes.

P: And William Stafford neither sings, in the Dylan Thomas sense, nor, surely, does he moan.

Yes, I feel implicit in this remark the idea that since I said the two things, I'm surely, by implication at least, I'm opting for one or the other, or I'm denying one and affirming the other, but in the poem—I feel like such an unreliable character in a poem that I can say something like "We have decided/to moan" and then drop it, just leave it, because I don't mean that for the rest of my life at all, I just mean that's a remark to make in order to get along to the next remark. And sometimes you make the kind of remark that you certainly don't want to stay with very long. I realize that I usually don't moan very much either.

P: Yes, and I was wondering if that was a reference to a particular kind or kinds of poetry that you find to be moaning.

Maybe I could make the move to identify something that hovers in the air, I think, for many writers now: despite this feeling about not wanting to be trapped by tradition, we all relate in our daily lives and in our writing lives to what's going on around us, so one of the things that's going on now is what I hear identified as the "confessional school," and the confessions often seem to be about the part of life that's more related to moaning than it is to singing. So in my poem (I now catch myself because of the context of these remarks here, being influenced by the presence of a very influential group of poets who are called "confessional poets") when I say "We have decided to moan," for the instant that I am making this remark I am aligning myself with them, but as I say, I drop this and try to get out of it, later.

P: The confessionals are very concerned with religion, and sin, and evil, and reading your poems I get the sense of a very moral person. Yet there is no sense of sin. There's much more of a sense of grace, of affirmation.

I feel an impulse to pursue two things in that. One is that, well I guess I can get it fast like this: even the conviction of sin is too presumptuous for a human being. It implies that you know more about what should be happening in the world than you in fact do know. We're so limited that to be that persuaded that we're sinful is a presumptuous act. So, I don't feel like feeling guilty because I don't know that much about it. For all I know I'm very good!

I think the topic could be tossed back and forth in various ways. When I hear someone that sure of how much they're suffering or how sinful they are, I think "How can a person so fallible know that much?" That's one reaction. The other thing that I'd like to pursue, even at the risk of blurring this first, is that I noticed you said, Al, so carefully, "You are a moral person, er, your poems say moral things." And I would like to preserve that distinction. The poems—you may say almost anything—my feeling is you say something in creative writing in order to find out what will be the result of saying this—so, frequently I find myself making emphatic and moral statements, but I don't mean them any more than that statement "We have decided to moan." I mean I try it out, see how it is. If the moral sound has an aesthetic effect, that's good. If it doesn't have an aesthetic effect, I guess I'll try a different kind of morals, is the feeling I have.

H: There is this dimension to art, isn't there? Someone said that it's awfully hard to believe "Song of Myself" and at the time believe the Old Testament, because the views of God in those two works are so different. But when we read them, we're really with them, aren't we?

Yes, this readiness to swivel from the Old Testament to "Song of Myself" is the kind of feeling, the kind of readiness, I've liked to cultivate in myself, and persuade my friends to give some kind of credence to. It's like the conversation we have with the world in our life is a conversation with many kinds of influences, and to read the Old Testament is to give the requisite allegiance to the part that you're reading at the time so that you'll be ready to take the next thing that comes along. To read "Song of Myself" is to give that requisite allegiance to that. But then, I feel like pulling back from both, and not saying either one, but probably saying "Neither. What shall we talk about now?"

H: Yes, yes. At the same time—Al used the word "moral"—at the same time I want to zero in a little bit

and say something like: I do get a sense of certain ver-
ities that ring true in Stafford's poems as I pursue them
through the books. Well, it almost sounds silly the way I
have to put it now, but love, *and the idea that the earth*
is a fine place to be—you don't pursue despair, and you
don't moan a great deal—I know you like to think of
your poems opposing one another, but there is a . . . we
can tell a Stafford poem.

Yes, I think there are tendencies. You know, no matter
how it feels to me from inside—it feels as if I can go in
any direction in every poem—but someone from outside
might say, "How come usually you go in *this* direc-
tion?" In which case I would have to say "Yeah, that's
right, well it just occurred to me to go in that direction
yesterday, too, come to think of it." But I have several
reactions about that recurrence of positive things in the
poems. Since it would be presumptuous for us to as-
sume with very much certainty that we're sinful or that
the world is one way or another, and since I sort of like
singing rather than moaning, and since love seems pleas-
ant to me and some other things seem unpleasant, I am
most unready to be hustled by those people around me
who say that suffering is more authentic than love. I
feel a great deal of reluctance about that.

H: When you were talking before, it occurred to me
that Wallace Stevens said that men have put into the
mouths of gods the only words they've ever spoken. So,
we do become presumptuous when we assume we know
just what kind of world this is.

Yes, when you say that, Bill, it makes me think that the
presumption—well, you have to put *some* words in their
mouths, so I'll have to back out and start over—so we

put some words in their mouths but even while we're doing it we think, well, some other words could come out too. I mean it's . . . I'm afraid . . . well, maybe I may as well not be afraid but just try to be brave about it, that I'm opting for a fairly wishy-washy kind of position. I mean, what did the gods really say? Well, uh, you'll have to ask somebody else, preferably a god, and I haven't met any of them.

H: Let me ask you this question about something that's been very much on my mind the last couple of years. You're predisposed toward affirmation—I don't know how to put it as gracefully as you did a minute ago. Do you think this is something we can opt for? I think of you and Richard Wilbur and other people who lead graceful and lovely lives, while I think of other people who do suffer a great deal and who perhaps end up very badly, like Delmore Schwartz and John Berryman. Do you think this is something that they had to become? Do you think you were blessed in being born with a naturally happy disposition, or bent toward what you are, or what?

Well some of this, Bill, I think, is, is, the choice part in the poems. I think. It's possible—I'm back with this feeling of freedom to go in any direction when writing—it's possible to write one way or another way. This I feel as I write. Your *life* and how you really feel inside yourself, or how they really felt inside themselves—I don't really know. I mean if we take someone like Berryman, whose outward life seemed a succession of disasters in some ways, I'm not really sure how he felt about that life. For all I know, those apparent debacles were very exhilarating. So I'd like to separate an estimate of how a person really feels inside. I mean I just don't know.

What is happiness to someone else? I don't know. I mean I try to judge by various gestures and sequences in their lives that my life is vacant of. It's like what does blue mean to someone else? I just know I can separate it out myself, but I don't know how they feel about it. But then there's another thing, too, about current writing. There's something dramatic—you can get a lot of mileage out of tragedy, and I think it's like an addiction to effective elements in art to indulge as a people, or as a group of writers, in one kind of literary invention. And I feel myself caught up in a time—this is probably a very local feeling on my part—caught up in a time in which those mileage-making elements in the arts have run away with the rest of our life. And so I do feel like taking a stand, deliberately, in the poems, and if I found myself always zeroing down to zero in my writing, I think that would finally get to me. I wouldn't want to avoid it, any day, or any time I have the impulse, because part of the fun of it is planing down to however you feel. But if I felt that way day after day, I wouldn't feel superior or inferior. I'd just feel lucky or unlucky. And it seems to me some people are awfully unlucky, and I don't want to turn to that kind of life in order to take part in a style of art. I just think it's unlucky—it's just too bad, some kinds of life.

P: Do you think that style of art is probably a dead end, in both senses of that word?

I don't know, but I was thinking of this, Al, when you were talking: maybe, it makes it sound as if engaging in that kind of art is a sacrifice. I mean you feel that's effective, that's the way you go—it sucks you into it, and you've created something for others. I feel more selfish than that, for one thing, and here's the chance to say something that might be a little bit graceful: I'm too *selfish* for that kind of sacrifice, if such it is. Now, I'm not sure. Is this on the point you were making, or not?

P: Well I was just thinking that after you have confessed X number of murders, sexual deviances, whatever it is, where do you go from there?

Actually it may be that we're letting ourselves be persuaded by something about overt content here. You may write something, a poem or a story or a novel, in which there will be all sorts of events and confessions, and it might seem to some readers that the effect of this poem, story, or novel depends on the nature of those things revealed (which I doubt). I think the effect of a poem, story, or novel depends much more on some kind of harmony or a consistency in the means and the ends of what's going on. So, it wouldn't make any difference how good or bad a character is, or how good or bad a writer says the self is—that's a superficial thing. What *really* is rewarding in the work is some kind of internal reinforcement, whatever is in the work. And I'd like to feel available—this is sort of like saying we could read the Bible or "Song of Myself" or anything else—I'd like to be available to go along with worthy company in any direction in my mind. It seems to me that's what art enables us to do. You know, we can accompany these *rash* explorers, even these suicidal explorers. I always hope their lives are not like that—I don't think their lives *need* to be like that, but in our dreams and in our thoughts we can be all sorts of extreme things.

H: When you mention the word "dream"—this is one of

the things "An Introduction to Some Poems" is about: in our poems, doing in them very often what our dreams do for us.

Yes, this has been down the center of our conversation, I think—the thing you touch on. That is, just as we don't choose our dreams—they choose us—I have this feeling that if we can get with ourselves somehow, and let the thing that we're doing at the moment when we are writing unfold, like a dream, with as little guidance as a dream has, it will somehow be, there will be more of ourselves in it than if we have made a prior commitment to some particular kind of poem or story or novel. So, we could talk about writing and the arts in many ways, but I think there's a little crucial distinction here. There are craftsmen who have learned what the editor of the *Ladies' Home Journal* likes to publish. That's one thing. I don't think that's what we're talking about, is it?

H: No, not at all. One of your poems ends, "Be, be, Buddha said."

Yes.

H: Kenneth Burke describes some of Roethke's early poems as unfolding in the present, something like that.

I see. Yes. I hadn't heard that.

H: You say in this poem "The authentic is a line from one thing/along to the next." And this poem is about the authentic in poetry, and in life. But how does a line get to the next line? And how do you, and you teach creative writing, how do you notice, say, distortion in a poem, or something that isn't right, or . . .

For one thing, I can imagine someone saying the opposite move, sort of like in a chess game, saying "Whaddaya mean 'The authentic is this,' it's really that." So the language is something I'm quite ready to trade on. I mean if anyone were to emphatically say to me "No it isn't," I would listen to that person because I, you're both pursuing something, left hand right hand finding it is sort of the feeling. So I want to be careful not to appear to be saying too much. But there is, I have a clue, I think, to forward motion in writing. And it is sort of like this: that there is something implicit in anything. I realize this may just be the reverberation of myself, and I'm conditioned that way. But it *feels* as if there's something implicit. So I get little nudges from even the syllables—it doesn't have to be the meaning of a word—it can be a syllable, or the beginning or end of a syllable or the fact that there isn't very much in the middle. *Anything.* So, whatever's implicit suggests the next thing, and if it suggests it to me, it may suggest it to someone else. I can't tell, so I just follow whatever nudges I feel, and it may be that later I'll find that I have company from someone else. This is one reason I started by saying there may be someone who says about the authentic "well, no it isn't." Well, if you happen to have some kind of survival percentage of positive nudges that you share with other people, then they say "that's good." Now, I don't want to insult other people, but if anybody says "that's good," I translate that to mean "that's the way I think, too." And we both may be way off according to god, or whatever.

H: Yes. But I'm a little unhappy about one thing now, and I know that will make you happy!

Yes.

*H: You were saying that you're pleased to follow the
company, whether it's the company of the* Old Testa-
ment *or the company of "Song of Myself."*

Yes.

*H: But we do have someone like Williams who says,
early, that we can't be eclectic anymore; we have to
choose a kind of poetry, and if we choose the poetry
of Eliot, we're heading toward the waste land, and we're
putting civilization back. And if you choose this new
poetry, this different poetry, then civilization has a
chance to survive on the planet, and we really do have
to make choices.*

I think of one good clear thing to say during this conver-
sation: Williams is too doctrinaire on this point. That's
one way to say it. And I'm interested, but I'm not con-
vinced when he says it. Then I'd like to be in a conver-
sation, and if T. S. Eliot were there that wouldn't mean
that I'd shut T. S. Eliot out from the rest of my life be-
cause I've listened to Williams. That isn't the kind of life
an intellectual leads. I would like to lead the kind of life
in which it would be possible for me to talk to Williams
at his most eloquent, and still be available for T. S.
Eliot's rejoinder. And the idea that civilization means
electing someone who is forceful, and current, and in
the vogue, is not my idea of how civilization goes on.

*P: I think probably one poem that illustrates that is
your poem called "Vocation," in a way, and if you
would read it we could . . .*

I'd be happy to read it. I even have enough realization
of what's in this to think I get what you're saying about

it. It wouldn't be true about all the poems, but I do remember this one.

Vocation

This dream the world is having about itself
includes a trace on the plains of the Oregon trail,
a groove in the grass my father showed us all
one day while meadowlarks were trying to tell
something better about to happen.

I dreamed the trace to the mountains, over the hills,
and there a girl who belonged wherever she was.
But then my mother called us back to the car:
she was afraid; she always blamed the place,
the time, anything my father planned.

Now both of my parents, the long line through the plain,
the meadowlarks, the sky, the world's whole dream
remain, and I hear him say while I stand between the two,
helpless, both of them part of me:
"Your job is to find what the world is trying to be."

I hadn't realized that here, again, we've been standing between the two, between Williams and T. S. Eliot! I'm just trying to find what the world is trying to be. Hmm. I'm glad you know my poems well enough to think of something that's relevant. . . .

Sometimes I think that a good way to be is like having a head in which ideas just roll around like a marble, any direction. You know, I turn this way and I'm with it, and I turn this way and I'm with it. And I think of a story about writing that connects to this. I read a biography of Niels Bohr. When he was a little kid in school, they tried to teach him to write according to the way teachers teach people to write: that everything should have a beginning, a middle, and an end; there are forms that one should follow. And little Niels

Bohr, in whose head ideas rolled around like marbles, couldn't learn how to end what he wrote. And I've memorized the last sentence in one of his themes. At the end he said, "And I would also like to mention aluminum."

H: That's good. That's good. And, you know, one of his friends was Werner Heisenberg. And that phrase, "the uncertainty principle," might mean, finally, that physically speaking even, even beyond these emotional nudges that we feel, that there just is a basic physical uncertainty in our universe, including the uncertainty, say, of the speed of light, which has always been the most certain of all things.

Yes, later is not yet now, that kind of feeling. Yes.

P: I'd like to get back to a couple of things that came up earlier, in terms of influences. We were talking about the moral stance. How much do you think your being a Quaker and conscientious objector has influenced your work?

I'm sure it has influenced my work, but part of that assurance, such as it is, comes from signals I get from the world around me that as a matter of fact where we come from, who we associate with, the kinds of things that we do all the time, *do* influence us, and the things you mention have been very much a part of my background, and are still part of my foreground, as a matter of fact. And I welcome it. I think one of the topics for us maybe when we all talk to other people who are engaged in the arts now—many of them are trying to shake a past. I mean they have a feeling of rebellion.

And when the marble in my head rolls that way I say "Yes, yes, I understand." But part of the time the marble rolls the other way and I say, "Well, why? It depends. It depends." And in my own life I have this feeling of not a past that is to be left because it's past, but only reluctantly would I give up the influence of my parents, the influence of any of those ideas that have been earlier in my life. I'm ready, when T. S. Eliot says so, or when Williams says so, or whatever, but I don't want to be overeager, I mean it's just a matter of going along with wherever I happen to be, too, and whatever I, too, happen to be.

H: Doesn't one of your poems say "I place my feet with care in such a world"? Do I have that line right?

That's the way I remember it, too, Bill. Yes.

H: Al and I have just recently discovered this lovely, this beautiful little book that you wrote after your experience as a conscientious objector—you spent four years in various camps in this country—

Yes, yes.

H: It first came out in 1947, and now we have a reprint of Down in My Heart *that we can get hold of. Do you see that experience, the four years of feeling sort of like a displaced person within your own country—have you defined for yourself what maybe that did to your self? Has it steeled you, that's the . . .*

Oh, when you say "steeled"—the syllable does something to me.

H: I mean I see you as a very gentle man, but also a man of very strong convictions, a strong man, at the same time.

I suppose four years in a concentration camp, wherever it is, would make a difference, but the reason I reacted to "steeled" is that if we're not careful—and that's why I place my feet with care in this world—if we're not careful, any extreme experience like being in a camp for four years, you know, drafted into it and held there, will so tilt us that we're not *ready*. It seems to me the intellectual life and the life of the arts depends on a kind of readiness, and so many of my friends who were in this experience were in fact locked into an attitude toward society that is very disquieting to me. I mean you can become addicted to losing fights with any society you're in, and I just feel nervous about it. I'm probably betraying more of that past in the way I respond to this, than in what I say about it. I feel nervous about overreacting to any experience.

P: In order to locate. This is 1974, April, and we're in the middle of a very difficult time in our national history. Our President may be impeached. How do you respond at this moment in history to the national experience?

Partly because of what's been said earlier I suddenly realize that I am able to make a remark that is consistent, and I'm afraid it's all too consistent with what I've said earlier. And that is that no matter what's happening in society for me, and I agree with you that these extreme things are imminent, perhaps, I still learn from the people around me, as a writer. I don't feel full of insights and ready to proclaim for sure, discoveries, but even under the extreme circumstances of being put into camp for four years, I found it interesting to talk to the people who were holding us there, you know, the bosses, and so I would have this feeling today that it's not a cops and robbers problem in society, it's a kind of mutual problem in society. You see I'm not giving any answer, but I'm trying to give an attitude toward what's going on. I don't locate the trouble in the bad guys so much as I do in some kind of phase that maybe we're all going through. I don't think this is very helpful, but it's an attitude.

H: How about a more specific question? Do you think this long, drawn-out Watergate investigation is generally good for the country or would we have been better off if...

No, no, I think it's good for the country. I feel very positive about all the reverberations.

P: This leads to a natural request for another poem, also, and that's a political poem. I'd like you to read "At the Bomb Testing Site," which is, in my feeling, a quiet protest poem rather than polemic.

Yes. I have a feeling, by the way—you said a quiet protest poem—if we could refine outward toward the edges of this attitude that we have sort of located here, I think it would be possible for me at the end of a long conversation in which we all identified our positions very carefully to say that every poem I have ever written is a quiet protest poem. You know, somewhere in it is this kind of "yes, but, Dr. Williams, yes, but, Mr. Eliot" kind of thing, and so protest becomes less like a doctrinaire position to take in opposition than it is like "what does somebody else have to say?" But when you talk you have to take a succession of still positions. It's sort of like a movie, you know, you're frozen, so here's where I'm frozen in this posture so I'll read this frozen posture protest poem.

At the Bomb Testing Site

At noon in the desert a panting lizard
waited for history, its elbows tense,
watching the curve of a particular road
as if something might happen.

It was looking for something farther off
than people could see, an important scene
acted in stone for little selves
at the flute end of consequences.

There was just a continent without much on it
under a sky that never cared less.
Ready for a change, the elbows waited.
The hands gripped hard on the desert.

H: Well, you've really zeroed in in that little poem.

I guess the lizard is placing its feet with care in such a world in that poem. I hadn't realized the relevance of that phrasing before.

H: It occurs to me that you have a line here—"under a sky that never cared less"—some of your poems, you know, just oppose that whole view of nature. In some of your poems the sky does seem to be involved with human beings. I think that fiction, not a fiction but there is a wavering going on in the Stafford canon there in regard to, you know . . .

Actually, I feel not an occupier of a salient position on this attitude, but maybe this is the sort of feeling a lot of us might have, but feeling that surely everyone would agree with me if we could talk long enough about this, and my feeling is, is both ways. I mean in life sometimes the wind is blowing in the same direction you're going, and sometimes it's blowing in another direction, and apparently it doesn't make a lot of difference to the wind, but it makes a difference to you. And so I have this kind of a strange feeling sometimes being identified as gentle, maybe because sometimes I don't feel that adjective is at all a crucial adjective. It's not our place, it's not within our power. Even if we think we're powerful, it's not within our power. You see there I begin to go over from the gentle into: it doesn't make any difference what anybody says what the sky does. I feel sort of on God's side when I say something like this.

H: This is a great big broad question, and almost a necessary one, so let me try it. Do you see your work as having essentially changed since you began? The split in some people's work has been very dramatic, and I certainly don't sense that.

Yes, yes, like you, probably, I've enjoyed reading, tracing the developments in people's work, maybe early Yeats and second, third, fourth, fifth Yeats. Something like that. My feeling is that it hasn't changed essentially, though I realize this may be an assessment made by virtue of my angle on the work. But what I see for everyone, even Yeats, if I could see well enough, would be right straight back down that life toward something that was implicit in the beginning. And I can be scholarly and do a book with two or three or four or five sections, too, and I like that, but part of what I'd like is that line right down the middle of that life. And down the middle of the life, as I see it (since I'd like to respond directly to this), is not the result of influences or developments along the way, so much as it is the result of early sustained harmonious relations with people around me, whose influence just doesn't pass away.

H: Yeats spent a lot of time revising his early poems. Now that's something you'd not care to do.

I don't think so because—although I can understand it, if I lean my head this way—on the other hand I realize that he might just as well be revising somebody else's poems, and preferably some poems of his own nearer where he is now, because he's not an expert on those older ones anymore.

P: What you said a little while ago reverts back to the first poem, also, that line that you talk about, going from here to there.

Aah, that's right. Must be an obsession of mine!

P: And it leads to a more specific question. Last night at your reading you said something to the effect that there are no great poets who have influenced you as much as the voice of your mother. I would just like you to comment on that, because we know so many poets who are spending millions of dollars with their psychiatrists attempting to get rid of their mothers.

Well, I suppose some mothers are more baleful than other mothers! That's one thing. And furthermore, aside from that—that's just one way to assess it—the other is that your life might have gotten into a tangle in which you've got to get rid of everything in order to get started again. This I think I can also conceptualize. But in saying this I was really trying to focus on an issue that often comes up with writers who are asked, "What great writer most influenced you?" And if the question is asked this way, you are very likely to be framed into it and come tearing out of the chute in a certain direction, identifying a writer because that's the way the question is phrased. But that's not really the question. In your life it is not what great person most influenced you, it is something nearer to you than that, and there is no writer great enough, in my opinion, to influence any human being as much as an early, sustained, even genetically harmonious influence like a mother's voice. Now I realize that if your mother happened to be Sappho, if that was possible, or whatever, then I have to qualify my statement. But nevertheless, it's the quality not of being Sappho but of being mother. Again, historically I'm sure that I'm *way* off base, but that's the crucial thing. It's a matter of nearness, and initial readiness, more than it is: "well I elect my great influence to be Shakespeare, say, or Thomas Hardy." And I lean my head and I understand when someone says "Yes, these phrases, this cadence I took from a verse of Yeats," or something like that. I understand, but what's inside those cadences you took not from a verse of Yeats, but that's the part that interests me, when you're right back, and I'm thinking of Roethke of course, you're right back there in balance, and it's the Roethke part that interests me.

H: And, by the way, he was so sorry that he'd said that.

Was he?

H: People came after him so often with that that he ended up denying the extent of the influence.

Well, you know, it's like a great big handle lying there that you can talk about. I can understand then his being disquieted.

H: It is so good, but it was treated in the wrong way for the rest of his life.

Yes, and I'm sorry to add to that burden.

H: Say, there's a little poem I'd like you to read. It's from Traveling Through the Dark *and it's called "B.C." I just have this feeling that we've done a lot of talking here, and we'd like you to read several poems.*

I ought to be able to find it in a hurry here. It'll be the shortest title. Yes.

B.C.

The seed that met water spoke a little name.

(Great sunflowers were lording the air that day;
this was before Jesus, before Rome; that other air
was readying our hundreds of years to say things
that rain has beat down on over broken stones
and heaped behind us in many slag lands.)

Quiet in the earth a drop of water came,
and the little seed spoke: "Sequoia is my name."

H: I like that poem very much, and it does something that so many Stafford poems do to me; that is, I find myself caught up in the anxieties of every day, but when I run into a Stafford poem it's like a poke in the ribs that says "Hey, it's a very big world, and it's a deep

world, and the wells go way down deep, and we have to
sort of pay attention to wider things."

Well, I suppose we all, no matter how free we feel when
we write, and I realize that all of us here do that, we
find ourselves characteristically coming back to a kind
of home base; and that poem, no matter how I would
assess it, I would have to say "Yes, I recognize a recur-
rent thing." To have a little seed say "Sequoia is my
name"—if I could revert to something we were talking
about, Al, it's almost as if I'm harking back to when I
said I feel every poem I ever wrote was, you know, was
some kind of mild little protest poem, so when the little
seed says "Sequoia," I feel it's in that category, but not
in a very aggressive way.

P: I think what I like about that poem too is that it's a
characteristic Stafford poem, that it takes a particular
kind of risk.

I wish I could learn more about this.

P: By using—let me put it this way: it seems to me
there are very few people who could pull off that kind
of poem, in waiting until the end to say "Sequoia is my
name."

Let me give a more blunt phrasing to this. It's a cheap
trick! Withhold information, then dribble it out when it
will do you the most good. After you've flimflammed
the reader as long as you think he could possibly stay
with you, say "Sequoia."

H: But I like that poem, even when I know what's
coming. . . . Yeah, I feel very much the same way Al
does. I don't think anyone *writing today sounds just*

the way you do. I would be hard put to define that Stafford voice, but some of it has to do with these little risks, and I think very often that a poem is successful sometimes in regard to the risks it takes.

If I could try to enhance this a little bit, or reinforce that statement, I've thought recently, when talking to many writers, that they are too reluctant to write their bad poems. Maybe it's related to that thing that started our conversation, that everyone has all kinds of dreams, everyone has all kinds of poems. Some people are so afraid of—maybe this is where the risk comes in—so afraid of writing a vulnerable, or an unfashionable, or just a kind of a cheap poem, that they're inhibited as if their dreams, their poems, get blocked for a long time. I don't know how to get out of this speech that I'm on, but I often have a feeling that people's standards are too high, and so the way I was going to enhance this was to say that some people don't have the nerve to write bad poems, but I do.

H: It's as though irony is the great tone since "Prufrock," since the teens, irony is the great tone, where so many writers, I think, the minute they become a little bit sincere, then their poem moves right in to undercut— that's the sense I have of so much poetry in our time.

Do you think that retaining that irony, which is so often a protection, could be inhibiting, could freeze you some place less than where you might get if you didn't always have to feel protective?

H: I think that's certainly true.

I realize bad things can happen when you don't have the

irony and everybody else thinks you should have had it.
It makes you pretty naive.

P: There's another dimension to it, to the Stafford poems that I like, and that is the quality of humor. So few people are writing poems that have an element of humor in them. We all take ourselves so seriously. So I'd like you to read "A Family Turn" which I think is a . . .

Yeah, I remember that poem.

P: . . . a nice example of this.

Surely, what you were saying about all of us taking ourselves seriously and so on—part of the time, yes, I understand this. Of course, in conversation we don't do that, hardly any of my friends are always taking themselves seriously, so it may be that we feel it's a part of nervousness: to go out into the big world one must go out with armor on. Well,

A Family Turn

All her Kamikaze friends admired my aunt,
their leader, charmed in vinegar,
a woman who could blaze with such white blasts
as Lawrence's that lit Arabia.
Her mean opinions bent her hatpins.

We'd take a ride in her old car
that ripped like Sherman through society:
Main Street's oases sheltered no one
when she pulled up at Thirty-first
and whirled that Ford for another charge.

We swept headlines from under rugs, names
all over town, which I learned her way, by heart,

and blazed with love that burns because it's real.
With a turn that's our family's own,
she'd say, "Our town is not the same"—

Pause—"And it's never been."

H: Louis Simpson, to follow up Al's point, has complained that there's a deadly solemnity in American poetry today and, again, it's very nice to be able to read your poetry and to smile on occasion.

I'd like to grab whatever distinction I can, so I'll try to live up to that one.

H: One of the things that people are interested in, and I'm certainly interested in this—because I find I'm happiest when I manage to write at a decent clip—is the fact that you're a very prolific writer. James Dickey, talking about your poems some years back, said that in general he suspected a muse that managed to inspire so often, but that in your case, what comes out for you is poetry, and it comes out naturally, and it's good that you write so much.

I don't like to be the kind who cherishes just certain kinds of remarks, but I do remember that Dickey was kind on that occasion. I don't really know about that, of course, but it is true that I write a lot. Well, earlier, Bill, you referred to something like "Talking along in our not-quite-prose way," and almost every day I write and so there's a lot written, and if my standards are low enough, I can say I write a lot of poems, and if my standards are as high as some people's, of course, I would dam up most of those so as not to be damned later by those who read them.

P: One quick question: is it true that you write five poems a day?

No, it is not true! Only four.

H: I've heard about three during a lunch hour once while you were having a sandwich!

P: We're approaching the end of our allotted time, and perhaps it would be good if we could end by asking you to read two last poems from your most recent book. How about "The Stick in the Forest" and "Report from a Far Place," which will bring us back to the opening poem, also?

The Stick in the Forest

A stick in the forest that pointed
where the center of the universe is
broke in the wind that started
its exact note of mourning
when Buddha's mother died.

Around us then a new crystal
began to form itself, and men—
awakened by what happened—
held precious whatever breathed:
we are all gestures that the world makes.

"Be, be," Buddha said.

And I'll just turn to the second one.

Report from a Far Place

Making these words things to
step on across the world, I
could call them snowshoes.

They creak, sag, bend, but
hold, over the great deep cold,
and they turn up at the toes.

In war or city or camp
they could save your life;
you can muse them by the fire.

Be careful, though: they
burn, or don't burn, in their own
strange way, when you say them.

Edited from a video-tape interview with William Stafford in
April 1974, sponsored by the Brockport Writers Forum, Depart-
ment of English, State University College, Brockport, New York
14420 © State University of New York.

IV
Toward This Book

Into the Cold World
Leaving the Workshop

It must have been the fall of 1950 when my wife
Dorothy and I, and our two tiny boys, pulled into Iowa
City in our old green Chevy, pulling the Stafford estate
in a two-wheeled trailer. Dorothy had a teaching job in
the city schools, and I had a grad assistantship paying
$700 a year and remission of fees. Our affluence en-
abled us to move into Quonset Park.

Those days, as I remember, the poetry workshop met
Monday afternoons for a couple of hours. Between fif-
teen and twenty poets would sit around the main room
in the barracks building beside the Student Union, and
Paul Engle would begin a tantalizing minuet of remarks,
and juggling multigraphed copies of student poems, and
establishing occasional insights that kept me excited and
hopeful. I had to learn the accomplishments and rela-
tions that structured the Engle remarks, which often
alluded to publications or rivalries that were out of my
ken. I soon caught some of the sly remarks. And from
the first I liked the Workshop, and throughout my two
years and one summer I served easy time.

Fiction workshop had about the same format, but it
was larger, and I found it less exciting: in poetry we were
always within a syllable or two of something over-
whelming; but in fiction there were discouraging num-

bers of pages elaborating a structure that—maybe, later—might come to something.

John Crowe Ransom was to visit Workshop one week, and a ludicrous thing happened. Our poems were submitted and then multigraphed in the office, and my poems for that week (Engle must have suffered from how many poems I poured into the sessions) got shaken down to two, and these for reasons of economy were pushed close together on one page. Mr. Ransom kindly fished my page out and began an analysis with so much finesse and care that I began to realize that I was the only one present who knew that the page was supposed to be *two* poems. That afternoon the new criticism welded my poems brilliantly together, and I was too gratified, and too timid, to pull them apart.

Dee Snodgrass and his wife Lila and their little girl lived in a quonset just beyond the garbage house from ours, and I profited from Dee's guidance; from the first, he seemed to be around Kenny's or The Airliner, or wherever the main gossip was, more than I; and he enjoyed the high regard of a number of our noted visitors—I remember Whittemore, and Penn Warren, and Jarrell. Jarrell in particular I remember for one of Dee's remarks—"It's fun to have a gee whizz critic now and then, after these austere visitors." (But I remember that Jarrell said, gee whizz, my poem was a nineteenth-century poem.)

It was along about this time that Dee began a pattern that was to make a great difference in his life: he stayed up later and later, making it necessary to sleep later and later; by the time the year was over he was living at night and Lila was keeping their child quiet through the day so that Dee could sleep.

Partly through Dee, and partly just through the closeness and informality of those Workshop days, I became pretty well acquainted with insiders, people who then or later enjoyed high places in the pecking order—and there always was a pecking order. Bill Belvin was an insider, and Donald Justice (whose insights I early learned to respect) was, and James B. Hall, and Don Petersen, and Leonard Woolf. And there was a girl whose talent gained Workshop respect—she confided to me during one time when the Romantics were getting their usual demolition, "But I *like* Shelley." No one else heard her, and she throve. Later, when Penn Warren visited, she was so excited that she spent her grad assistant pay for a dress to wear to class. Warren made his greatest impression on me when he glanced magisterially through several pages of poetry manuscript and said, "I do not understand these poems." I had been studying Brooks and Warren in order to be able to understand *any* poems.

Shapiro came, and the poets had a party at the Engle place in Stone City. For Dorothy and me it was a wondrous time—those rolling hills looking just like the pictures, and the big stone barn, and the rooms full of writers. I even had a chance to ask Shapiro something that had been troubling me. He was editing *Poetry* at the time, and I was afraid that my habit of sending stacks of poems to editors might lead them to rate me by the poems they liked least. Shapiro said, "Don't worry—we get bad poems from everyone."

Now I remember an influence that was always present at Iowa during those years, not heavily present, but continuous, and so remote now that it might be missed and thus left out of assessments that could be puzzling for the omission: many students then were veterans. They were back from a Just War. And I was a pacifist. At the gatherings, some of the zing of the sociability came from that shared past, for the others. They told me my stand was all right, and Dorothy and I caught up social momentum by attending Friends Meeting, held often in the Student Union on First Day.

The student with social concerns most like mine was George Bluestone. He was very successful while at Iowa; I believe lately he has gone astray into film. I remember that one time he sold a story to *The Atlantic*, and was holding a party to celebrate his check. When he telephoned Norm Springer to invite him, Springer said, "Oh, George, don't you know that news of your success is ruining my enjoyment of dinner?" This feeling of rivalry was all around us, partly a joke, but felt. I remember going over to the library to look at James B. Hall's thesis, a collection of short stories—I intended to try for my degree with a book. I felt frightened when I read the stories—they were so good. And other writers were in the library studying like mad; for a Ph.D. we could use our writing for the thesis, but we had to match those fanatics in the regular English department, on the tests. The attrition rate was high. Many writers settled for various adjustments, and no doubt for most the big inducement was the thought of a strike in publishing.

During my second year my way was eased by the friendship and guidance of a lucky sequence of teachers. Engle forgave me the spate of poems. Ray West was reassuringly there. And Walter Clark came in to teach and to share his great sociability. He was to read his story "The Wind and Snow of Winter" at the first meeting of the fiction workshop. When he finished, he was asked about his revisions in the story, the craft that went into it. He held still and considered and then said something like—"It's just a tale. I might have changed a few words."

Herb Wilner came over to our quonset and said Clark had consented to come over for dinner, and they didn't know whether they could adequately entertain him. Clark came, and late, late—far into the morning hours— he was telling his wonderful tales, relaxed, at home.

By the end of that second year, our family had become Iowans. We loved the place. We had packed the two-wheel trailer and tied the boys' little car on top of the load. I hurried from my orals, crossed the river, passed where Dee used to live, past the garbage house— and there was Dorothy coming to meet me, pulling the boys in their wagon: Paff, on the orals committee, an ogre, they said, who tripped up writers on their Old English, had telephoned to let Dorothy know I had made it.

Our sky is still fastened onto the Iowa sky.

UNDER DISCUSSION
David Lehman, General Editor
Donald Hall, Founding Editor

Volumes in the Under Discussion series collect reviews and essays about individual poets. The series is concerned with contemporary American and English poets about whom the consensus has not yet been formed and the final vote has not been taken. Titles in the series include:

On Louise Glück: Change What You See
edited by Joanne Feit Diehl
On James Tate
edited by Brian Henry
Robert Hayden
edited by Laurence Goldstein and Robert Chrisman
Charles Simic
edited by Bruce Weigl
On Gwendolyn Brooks
edited by Stephen Caldwell Wright
On William Stafford
edited by Tom Andrews
Denise Levertov
edited with an introduction by Albert Gelpi
The Poetry of W. D. Snodgrass
edited by Stephen Haven
On the Poetry of Philip Levine
edited by Christopher Buckley
James Wright
edited by Peter Stitt and Frank Graziano
Anne Sexton
edited by Steven E. Colburn
On Louis Simpson
edited by Hank Lazer
On the Poetry of Galway Kinnell
edited by Howard Nelson
Robert Creeley's Life and Work
edited by John Wilson
On the Poetry of Allen Ginsberg
edited by Lewis Hyde
Reading Adrienne Rich
edited by Jane Roberta Cooper
Elizabeth Bishop and Her Art
edited by Lloyd Schwartz and Sybil P. Estess